RHYMING TECHNIQUES

Songwriting: Essential Guide to Rhyming

A Step-by-Step Guide to Better Rhyming and Lyrics

Pat Pattison

Berklee Press
Director: Dave Kusek
Managing Editor: Debbie Cavalier
Marketing Manager: Ola Frank
Sr. Writer/Editor: Jonathan Feist

ISBN 0-7935-1181-X

1140 Boylston Street
Boston, MA 02215-3693 USA
(617) 747-2146

Visit Berklee Press Online at
www.berkleepress.com

DISTRIBUTED BY

HAL•LEONARD®
CORPORATION
7777 W. BLUEMOUND RD. P.O. BOX 13819
MILWAUKEE, WISCONSIN 53213

Visit Hal Leonard Online at
www.halleonard.com

BERKLEE PRESS, BOSTON 02215.
COPYRIGHT © 1991 BY BERKLEE COLLEGE OF MUSIC. ALL RIGHTS RESERVED.

CONTENTS

Pat Pattison has been teaching lyric writing and poetry at Berklee College of Music since 1975. He played a central role in developing Berklee's unique songwriting major, the first complete songwriting degree offered anywhere. Doctoral work in philosophy at Indiana University and a Master of Arts in Literary Criticism "... gave me wonderful tools for digging into lyrics to see what makes them work." In addition to his work for TV and film, as well as numerous clinics and workshops, Pat writes monthly articles for *Home and Studio Recording* magazine.

FOREWORD

This is not a general book in lyric writing. It has a very specific purpose: *to help you find better rhymes and use them more effectively.*

If you have written lyrics before, maybe even professionally, and you want to take a new look or gain even greater control and understanding of your craft, this book could be just the thing for you.

If you have never written lyrics before, this book will help. You won't have a chance to develop bad habits.

Rhyme is one of the most crucial areas of lyric writing. The great lyricists have at least this in common: they are skilled rhymers. This book will give you control over rhyming. It gives you the technical information necessary to develop your skills completely; to make rhyme work for rather than against you.

You can work completely through this book in two or three sittings. If you do the exercises, you will understand it the first time through. After that, use it only for reference.

You will need a rhyming dictionary. I use *The Complete Rhyming Dictionary*, edited by Clement Wood (Doubleday) as my source. I suggest you use it too. However, you can easily apply the information in this book to your own rhyming dictionary.

INTRODUCTION
DO I HAVE TO RHYME?

Songs are made for ears, not for eyes. Because people *listen* to songs, you must learn to write for eyeless ears. So many times rhyme seems like your enemy. Because it is so hard to use rhyme and still sound natural and genuine, most songwriters go through a "trying not to rhyme" phase. Too often, rhyme seems to pull you in a wrong direction, either

1. toward something that sounds unnatural, or
2. toward something cliché.

Both drain the blood out of your lyric.

1. *Something Unnatural*

How many appeals have gone "to the stars above" — how many emotions have flown in on "the wings of a dove?" Those countless stars and doves have every right to feel like teenagers who get attention only because they hang out with someone who rhymes with "love." They aren't really wanted for themselves.

The need to rhyme has certainly held the shotgun at many an improbable wedding. You may have been to a few yourself. . .

Sometimes the search for rhyme is even more destructive. Everyone has been in this situation: trying to find a way to connect words like

> liege
>
> besiege.

(No problem with cliché here.) Unless you were writing a comedy version of King Arthur or Robin Hood, you might never face this particular problem, but you have faced it in other ways many times. You will face it again.

"Besiege" is a transitive verb — you must use a Direct Object like "the castle" to complete its sense. Putting a Transitive Verb at the end of a phrase inverts the natural sentence order:

> He swore an oath unto his liege
>
> Tomorrow the castle he would besiege

You can pull your poetic license out of your back pocket all you want to, but you won't make the phrase sound any more natural. Of course, the natural syntax is

> He swore an oath unto his liege
>
> Tomorrow he would besiege the castle.

You might try

> He swore to his liege as a loyal vassal
>
> Tomorrow he would besiege the castle.

The first phrase is ambiguous. Is the liege the vassal? Even though "liege/besiege" are in the same internal spot, the meaning is obscured. This is better:

> To his liege he swore as a loyal vassal
>
> Tomorrow he would besiege the castle.

This is a lot of twisting in the wind for a rhyme. And you still didn't get

> liege
>
> besiege

in a rhyming position. The problem is familiar to anyone who has worked with rhymes, especially where only a few rhymes are available. For "liege" there is only

> besiege
>
> siege

Fortunately, "siege" is a noun.

> He swore an oath unto his liege
>
> To lay the castle under siege

A lucky escape.

2. *Something Cliché*

Having only a few rhymes available can cause even worse problems. Too often the available rhymes have been used so much that they are cliché. Have you ever tried to rhyme "love"? Or "desire"? Try for a minute. Make a list for each one.

> love   desire

I thought of "inspire." Alas, it turns into the Transitive Verb problem. It threatens to sound unnatural:

> You fill me with a strong desire
>
> Heat like this you can inspire

Using cliché rhymes is pretty risky business. Most likely your listener will start napping as soon as it is clear that you intend to use one of these old war horses. Unfortunately, English is full of them. Faced with these two problems,

1. using something that sounds unnatural, or
2. using cliché rhymes

you might be tempted to chuck rhyme altogether.

The problem is, refusing to rhyme hurts a lyric more than it helps it. This is not true in poetry, but remember, poetry is for the eye too. Rhymes in a lyric are the ear's roadsigns just like lines in poetry are the eye's roadsigns. In the time of the troubadour when poetry was oral, it always rhymed. It was made for the ear, not the eye.

There is a big difference between these two systems.

> 1. I've got a COLD SPOT in my heart
>
> Just for you
>
> Just for you
>
> It doesn't matter what you try
>
> Ain't no fire getting in
>
> I've got a COLD SPOT in my heart
>
> Just for you

2

2. I've got a COLD SPOT in my heart

    Just for you

    Just for you

    It doesn't matter what you do

    Ain't no fire getting through

    I've got a COLD SPOT in my heart

    Just for you

You can feel the difference. The rhymed version has punch and sarcasm. The unrhymed version doesn't. Yet both versions have approximately (maybe even exactly) the same meaning.

The decision is *not* between rhyming and not rhyming. The only decision is to learn how to rhyme more effectively.

Rhyme can be your best friend, your biggest help in leading all those eyeless ears through your lyrics. Or it can be your enemy. I want to show you how to make rhyme your friend. That is why you should work your way through this book. Carefully.

CHAPTER ONE
RHYME IS YOUR FRIEND

SHAKING HANDS

Rhyme is a connection between the sounds of syllables, not words. Only the last syllables rhyme in

under*wear*

re*pair*

The other syllables,

under

re

do not figure in at all.

When two syllables rhyme, it means three things:

1. The syllables' *vowel sounds* are the same

w*ea*r

p*ai*r

Even though these syllables' vowels have different letters, they make the same sound in these words. Only your ears count, not your eyes.

2. The sounds *after* the vowels (if any) are the same,

ea*r*

ai*r*

(As you can see by the "ea" in "wear" and "ear," sometimes the same letters sound different in different contexts.)

"(If any)" is important because syllables don't always have consonants after their vowel sounds, as in

disa*gree*

refe*ree.*

3. The sounds *before* the vowels are different.

*w*ear

*p*air

This third characteristic is important. It shows that rhyme works by the basic musical principle of tension /resolution: difference moving into sameness. When you hear a rhyme,

*w*ear   *gr*ee

*p*air   *r*ee

your ear notices that, in spite of the difference at the *beginnings* of the syllables, they end up sounding alike!

Beginnings of rhymed syllables have to be different so your ear will notice the similar sounds at the end. Otherwise, your ear will pick up only repetition, not rhyme. When you hear a cheerleader yell

go! go! go! go! go!

you pay attention to the repetition, not to the sounds of the syllables. No one in the stadium thinks "Hey! Those syllables sound the same!"

When the beginnings of syllables are the same, the syllables cannot rhyme. This is called an IDENTITY:

> fuse
>
> con*fuse*

It is not a rhyme. Your ear does not pay attention to the sounds of the syllables. There is no tension, no "difference" to be resolved by sameness.

> peace   lease
>
> piece   po*lice*

These words do not call attention to their sounds either, because their syllables do not resolve difference into sameness. The same sounds are repeated, just like a cheerleader's yell. But try

> peace   piece
>
> lease   police

These are a big difference from the Identities above them. There is also a big difference between these two lists:

1. birth*place*, common*place*, mis*place*, place, re*place*
2. ace, brace, chase, erase, face, disgrace, resting place

Say them aloud. Your ear does not focus on the sounds in the first list, but is drawn like a magnet to the sounds in the second list. In the first list you hear simple repetition. In the second list you hear the sound of music — or, rather, of tension /resolution.

Look at the three conditions again.

1. The syllables' *vowel sounds* are the same
2. The sounds *after* the vowels (if any) are the same,
3. The sounds *before* the vowels are different.

When syllables meet all three of these conditions, call it PERFECT RHYME. Later I will show you other kinds of rhyme besides PERFECT RHYME.

MASCULINE RHYMES/FEMININE RHYMES

Most rhymes, including PERFECT RHYMES, belong to one of two categories. Never to both. Every rhyme is either MASCULINE or FEMININE. (We will conveniently ignore three-syllable rhymes, at least for now.)

Here are some MASCULINE RHYMES:

> command
>
> land
>
> understand
>
> expand
>
> strand

Here are some FEMININE RHYMES:

> commanding
>
> landing
>
> understanding
>
> expanding
>
> stranding

As you can see, the difference is in the way they end.

MASCULINE RHYMES are either one-syllable words, or words that end on a *stressed* syllable:

comm**á**nd

land

underst**á**nd

exp**á**nd

strand

FEMININE RHYMES *always* end on an unstressed syllable. They are *always* two-syllable rhymes. (Masculine rhymes are one-syllable rhymes.)

comm**á**nding

l**á**nding

underst**á**nding

exp**á**nding

str**á**nding

Look at the stressed syllables in the FEMININE RHYMES above and you will see that they are all PERFECT RHYMES:

m**á**nd　ing

l**á**nd　ing

st**á**nd　ing

p**á**nd　ing

str**á**nd　ing

Stressed syllables, whether in FEMININE RHYMES or MASCULINE RHYMES, create rhyme's tension and resolution.

· The unstressed ending syllables above are all IDENTITIES, which is normal for Feminine Rhyme. These IDENTITIES only continue the resolution. Unstressed syllables of FEMININE RHYMES are usually IDENTITIES, but they do not have to be.

comm**á**nder

underst**á**nd her

exp**á**nd me

str**á**nd thee

Call these pairs above MOSAIC RHYMES, since they are put together with syllables of different words, like stained glass pieces in a church window.

Some words end on *secondary stress*, a syllable that, while it is not the *primary* stress in the word, is stronger than the syllables around it. Use "//" to mark secondary stress.

ap–pr**é**–ci–**à**te

Listen to it. You can tell by the pitch of the last syllable that it is stronger than the syllable before it. You cannot treat it as Feminine Rhyme, since its second-last syllable is the unstressed syllable. All Feminine Rhymes have a stressed second-last syllable, or at least their second-last syllable is stronger than the last syllable.

You have two choices when you rhyme "appreciate":

1.　You can treat it as a one-syllable Masculine Rhyme.

appreciate

fate

relate

Even better, you can rhyme it with other secondary stresses:

appréci*ate*

navi*gate*

compen*sate*

2.   You can treat it as a three-syllable rhyme. (Here as a Mosaic):

ap *pre ci ate*

quiche he ate

These three-syllable rhymes are still Masculine, since their last syllable is more stressed than the one before it. The somersaults you have to turn for these little gems are worth it only if you are writing comedy. They sure do dance.

FINDING RHYMES

Occasionally when I've asked writers what rhyming dictionary they use, some have been indignant, as though to say, "I do not cheat. I am self-sufficient." Others have looked at me sadly, as if hoping that someday I will abandon my artificial crutch and get in touch with my creative inner self.

Use a rhyming dictionary. This is one place where self-reliance and rugged individualism is silly. Finding rhymes is almost never a creative act. It is a purely mechanical search. On those few occasions where it is creative (finding mosaic rhymes, for example), a rhyming dictionary can still stimulate the creative process.

The self-reliant writer who thinks rhyming is a spontaneous expression of personal creativity can usually be seen gazing into space, lost somewhere in the alphabet song, "discovering" one-syllable words. This "alphabet process" is certainly at least as artificial as a rhyming dictionary. Nothing about it is creative or pure, nor is it spontaneous. The worst part of it is its inefficiency.

Try it. Clench your jaw, assume your best self-reliant posture (legs planted, hands on hips, staring determinedly beyond the horizon) and come up with rhymes for "attack."

Here is a typical result:

back	quack
hack	rack
jack	sack
lack	tack (oops!)
mack	wack
knack	zach
pack	

Mentally running through the alphabet misses in two areas:

1.   It misses words that begin with more than one consonant.
Here are some you might have missed:

black	smack
brac	snack
clack	stack
crack	thwack
plaque	track
shack	whack
slack	

2. It misses multi-syllable words ending on the rhyme sound. Here are more you might have missed:

> aback
>
> almanac
>
> bareback
>
> bivouac
>
> blackjack
>
> cardiac
>
> egomaniac
>
> haystack
>
> kleptomaniac . . .

If you're going to use an artificial process, at least use an efficient one!

Finding rhymes is mechanical. Once you have found out what is available, the real creative process begins: *using* rhyme. And the more alternatives you have to choose from, the more room you have to be creative. Anyone can find a rhyme; not everyone can use rhyme creatively.

The Complete Rhyming Dictionary, edited by Clement Wood (Doubleday), is the best rhyming dictionary around. It divides rhymes into Masculine, Feminine, and three-syllable rhymes. It is organized phonetically by vowel sound, italicizes archaic words, and is as complete in its listings as something in print can be. (Nothing can keep up with current slang. But you can write those in.) Get it in hardcover so it will last.

EXERCISE 1: WALK TO A BOOKSTORE AND BUY YOUR RHYMING DICTIONARY.

USING YOUR RHYMING DICTIONARY

There are three sections. The first lists masculine Rhymes; the second, Feminine Rhymes; the third, three-syllable rhymes. Each section is organized alphabetically according to the vowels, a, e, i, o, u.

To find a rhyme, ask two questions:

1. *Is the word I want to rhyme Masculine or Feminine?*

The answer will direct you to Section One or Section Two. Now ask the next question:

2. *What is the vowel sound of the stressed syllable?*

Look at the bottom of any pages. You will see the following list:

āle, câre, ădd, ärm, åsk; mē, hēre, ĕnd; īce, ĭll; ōld, ôr, ŏdd, oil fŏŏt, out; ūse, ûrn, ŭp; THis, thin;

This is your vowel index. It uses familiar words to help you identify the sounds, and gives you phonetic markings over each vowel.

Look up "attack." First, it is Masculine: (attáck). You will find it in Section One.

Look at the phonetic index for the vowel sound of the stressed syllable "tack." It is the short ă, as in "add."

The rhyming dictionary lists by vowel and ending consonant. You will find it under the column headed "AK." All Masculine words ending with short ă + "k" are listed in the column. Most are Perfect Rhymes for "attack." Some are Identities.

Try the Feminine: (hóllow). It will be in Section Two.

Look in the phonetic index for the vowel sound of the stressed syllable "hol." (Yes. The short ŏ as in "ŏdd.") Look in the Feminine section under the vowel "Ŏ." (The fourth part of the Feminine section.) Look alphabetically for "ŎL + o."

The stressed syllable is in CAPS and the unstressed syllable is in lower case. You will find "hollow" plus other words, "Apollo, swallow, wallow," among others.

Practice using your rhyming dictionary for a while. You may be slow at first, but like anything else, you will get better with practice.

EXERCISE 2: USING YOUR RHYMING DICTIONARY, FIND TWO INTERESTING RHYMES FOR EACH OF THE FOLLOWING WORDS.

1. love:

2. leadership:

3. blessed:

4. attendant:

5. crude:

6. Athena:

7. cripple:

8. grease:

9. stroked:

10. filet:

CHAPTER TWO
EXCHANGING BUSINESS CARDS

You have been introduced. Now find out what Rhyme does for a living. Its business card reads:

> RHYME:
> 1. I spotlight ideas.
> 2. I connect ideas.
> 3. I create motion.

We will look at the first two. My book, *Managing Lyric Structure*, deals with creating motion.

1. *Rhyme spotlights ideas*

The rhyming positions are at the ends of phrases. Because they control structure, end-phrase positions are always important. When the ends of phrases rhyme, the phrase-end position takes on extra importance. Here's why.

1. It is followed by a grammatical pause. This lets the lyric's idea "ring on" during the silence.

2. On the musical side of the song, there is usually a musical rest with the phrase rest, creating an end to a melodic phrase as well.

3. Since it is the end of a musical phrase, a melodic or harmonic signal usually will tell you what to expect next. This special musical function calls even more attention to the spot.

4. When there is rhyme in the phrase-end position, it has a special feature: it will *sound like* other words, again focusing attention on the position.

You can see that the rhyme position at phrase-end attracts a lot of attention. It is a HOT SPOT. This HOT SPOT gives you an opportunity: if you put important ideas there, they will have a better chance of being noticed. You will be able to get your ideas across better. Look at these lists:

1.			2.		
	me	a		crash	a
	do	b		thud	b
	be	a		mash	a
	you	b		blood	b
	know	c		drip	c
	so	c		slip	c

They both have the same rhyme scheme. The first one is a real snore. The second spreads clouds of imagery. It suggests a story all by itself. Imagine what might happen if you had whole phrases.

Try something. Pick out two of your old lyrics and list your rhyme words on a sheet of paper. It is revealing (and too often depressing) to see how little attention you pay to the most powerful positions you have to work with. If your lists are dull rather than interesting, you are not getting the most out of your rhyming position. Get into the habit of noticing what you put there.

If you can get a good idea of a lyric's meaning just from HOT SPOT information, you are using your rhyming positions effectively.

Look carefully at these lists. Imagine a story for them. The rhymes carry the ideas almost by themselves.

nights	stair	means	kegs
lights	hair	limousines	dregs
green	undone	drive	clear
seventeen	twenty-one	thirty-five	year

Now look at the full lyric.

> When I was seventeen IT WAS A VERY GOOD YEAR
> IT WAS A VERY GOOD YEAR for small town girls
> And soft summer *nights*
> We'd hide from the *lights*
> On the village *green*
> When I was *seventeen*
>
> When I was twenty-one IT WAS A VERY GOOD YEAR
> IT WAS A VERY GOOD YEAR for city girls
> Who lived up the *stair*
> With perfumed *hair*
> That came *undone*
> When I was *twenty-one*
>
> When I was thirty-five IT WAS A VERY GOOD YEAR
> IT WAS A VERY GOOD YEAR for blue blooded girls
> Of independent *means*
> We'd ride in *limousines*
> Their chauffeurs would *drive*
> When I was *thirty-five*
>
> But now the days are short, I'm in the autumn of the year
> And now I think of my life as a vintage wine
> From fine old *kegs*
> From the brim to the *dregs*
> It poured sweet and *clear*
> IT WAS A VERY GOOD *YEAR*
>
> — Ervin Drake, "Very Good Year"

These rhymes really communicate the lyric's meaning. By the time you add in the other phrase-end words, the story is practically complete.

EXERCISE 3: FROM YOUR RECORD COLLECTION FIND TWO LYRICS, ONE THAT USES THE HOT SPOT EFFECTIVELY, AND ONE THAT DOES NOT. LIST THE RHYMES.

Title 1 _____   Title 2 _____

HOT SPOT WORDS: HOT SPOT WORDS:

Since your rhyme position has hot lights shining on it, you had better put interesting ideas there. Your worst enemies are *empty rhymes* and *cliché rhymes*.

You have already seen some *empty rhymes* :

> me
>
> do
>
> be
>
> you
>
> know
>
> so

EXERCISE 4: HOW ABOUT SOME CLICHÉ RHYMES? YOU FILL IN THE BLANKS. DO NOT USE YOUR RHYMING DICTIONARY. JUST GRAB THE FIRST RHYME THAT YOU CAN THINK OF.

hand/ _____	heart/ _____
fire/ _____	alone/ _____
care/ _____	arms/ _____
feel/ _____	eyes/ _____
cry/ _____	call/ _____
walk/ _____	only/ _____
above/ _____	met/ _____
burn/ _____	true/ _____

None of these words are empty. They mean *something* . But when you pair them with their predictable mates, they bland off to nowhere. (I got as answers: "understand, desire, there, real, die, talk, love, learn, apart, telephone, charms, realize, all or wall, lonely, regret or forget, you/do/ blue/ through/ new.") These pairs all cause sleeping sickness.

Your goal is to find a cure for the infection.

Start by looking up the words from EXERCISE FOUR in your rhyming dictionary and see if you can do better.

2.   *Rhyme connects ideas*

Look at these words:

> lust
>
> burn

These two ideas connect, at least as metaphors. Other ideas rush in: "consume, torment, hot . . ." But besides having four letters, the syllables have no connection at all. Rather, your attention stays focused on their meanings, their metaphorical connection. The connection could be strengthened if the syllables had something in common: if they sounded alike.

> desire
>
> fire

Not only do these ideas connect, but so do their syllables, creating a "double whammy": a connection between ideas plus a connection between sounds. Unfortunately the rhyme is a cliché rhyme. It has been used so much that its power to provoke vivid ideas is gone. But look at this:

> passion
>
> ashes

No more cliché. They may not be Perfect Rhymes, but their sonic connection is undeniable.

EXERCISE 5: FOR EACH OF THE WORDS BELOW, FIND A RHYME WORD THAT SHARES AN IDEA IN COMMON WITH ITS PARTNER. DO NOT USE CLICHÉ RHYMES. TRY TO HOOK EACH WORD UP WITH A RHYME PARTNERS THAT CREATE A "DOUBLE WHAMMY" — A CONNECTION ON BOTH THE LEVEL OF MEANING AND SOUND. USE YOUR RHYMING DICTIONARY.

burn/	_____	dream/	_____
scold/	_____	grip/	_____
scorn/	_____	trance/	_____
break/	_____	leave/	_____
affair/	_____	alarm/	_____
school/	_____	past/	_____

When you use your rhyming dictionary in such a focused way — looking for words that connect ideas — it is a real help.

Some of your rhyming pairs above might suggest other ideas. "Scold/hold" could suggest an argument, complete with making up afterwards. (Or it might have been a telephone call.) "Break/mistake" could be Mom's favorite lamp, perhaps followed by "scold/hold." A rhyme often suggests some further idea. That is one of its powers and benefits.

Before, when you have written lyrics, you've waited until you already have a phrase to match before you looked for a rhyme. As you looked at each possibility, you tried to find ways to match them with your original word. As you know, some pretty strange ideas can come from this process, some more workable than others. Looking for a rhyme for "desperado" could lead you to something like this:

> Slicker than a desperado
>
> He moves in smooth and splits staccato
>
> Steals your heart and runs for cover
>
> Leaves a trail of broken lovers

What this process shows is the power of rhyme to make you think of new ideas. A rhyming dictionary can actually stimulate the creative process.

EXERCISE 6: WRITE A SECTION OF TWO TO FOUR LINES USING THE RHYMES BELOW. TRY TO MAKE SERIOUS CONNECTIONS. HUMOR IS EASY TO COME BY, SINCE MIS-MATCHES ARE OFTEN FUNNY.

1. net/duet

2. choke/baroque

3. lice/price

4. dark/mark

5. trees/knees

Even with your rhyming dictionary in hand, too often no good rhymes are available. Connections sound silly or far-fetched. You feel like you have to force ideas to rhyme, when the opposite should be happening. It makes you want to go into your "I–don't–want–to–rhyme" stage. Work with this:

> I'm sick of all this risky business
>
> I want to play it safe. . .

To get a third phrase, you might try to rhyme "business." Look in your rhyming dictionary in the feminine section under "IZ ness."

Oops. No words rhyme with it. Now you have two choices.

1. Since it is feminine, find a *mosaic rhyme*, or,
2. Don't rhyme it.

Look in the masculine section under short ĭ + "z." These seem the best of the short list: fizz, friz, his, is, quiz, 'tis, and whiz. Fizzness? Frizness? Hisness? Isness? Quizness? Tisness? Whizness? There are some faint sparks, but all seem to smack of forced comedy that promise only self-consciously "look–at–me–I–can't–find–a–rhyme" humor.

Remember, feminine rhymes do not necessarily have Identities in their unstressed syllables. Look in the masculine section under short ĕ + "s." Of course, only one-syllable words will do.

> Bess
>
> bless
>
> chess
>
> dress
>
> fess

>> guess
>>
>> jess
>>
>> less (eureka)
>>
>> mess (hmmm)
>>
>> press
>>
>> stress

Most of these are too strong to work as the unstressed syllable in a feminine mosaic. You need something with the same stress pattern as

>> busi ness

With most of the choices, for example,

>> his guess

You will end up with

>> hís guéss

or, even worse,

>> hĭs guéss.

Both of these sound forced and again, self-consciously funny. But "less" could really work, since it actually could be unstressed.

>> quizless
>>
>> fizzless

Try.

>> I'm sick of all this risky business
>>
>> I want to play it safe
>>
>> I'll learn to drink my tonic fizzless

Of course, "drink my tonic" is the linking idea that allows "fizzless" to work. It seems a little on the light and forced side, but it seems to be one of the few possibilities. (Try working with a few of the others.)

The key to what will happen in the third phrase is often what happens in the fourth. Before you decide anything for sure, see what is available for "safe."

>> chafe
>>
>> strafe
>>
>> waif

Ick. Even if you wanted "strafe," it is a transitive verb needing a direct object to complete it. (Remember "besiege?")

>> chafe
>>
>> waif

Try "chafe" first.

>> I'm sick of all this risky business
>>
>> I want to play it safe
>>
>> I'll learn to drink my tonic fizzless
>>
>> Where no one makes me chafe (?)

Ugh! This is downright gruesome, like an underwear commercial. You could keep trying to use "chafe" in a more imaginative way, or to lead up to it with a better idea. I don't see much hope.

I don't see much hope for "waif" either. You might try something like

> I'm sick of all this risky business
>
> I want to play it safe
>
> Or die a helpless waif

Then try to write a different (unrhymed) third phrase.

The problem is not the approach to "chafe," nor is it that "waif" needs to fit more naturally. Neither word has much promise. Yet lyricists often spend valuable energy and creativity trying to create silk purses with words like these.

The problem, as usual, is in picking "business" and "safe" without much forethought.

This is a typical problem, the kind that makes you want to re-enter your "I–don't–want–to–rhyme" stage.

Here is PART of the solution:

Look hard before you pick your friends.

CHAPTER THREE
GETTING REFERENCES

If you are lonely and you want to make friends, you should go places where you are likely to find people you have things in common with. Maybe go to a concert. Even a library. If you look around for a while in the right kind of place, something may click.

When you start writing your lyric before you think about rhymes, it's like looking for friends in places where you don't fit in. You might meet someone with things in common, but you could improve the odds by looking in places you like . . .

WORKSHEETS

The trick is to look for rhymes *before* you start to write. It is not as hard as it sounds:

1. Focus your lyric idea as clearly as you can.
2. Make a list of words that fit your idea.
3. Look up those words in your Rhyming Dictionary, and make lists of rhyme words that fit your idea.

Start with our old idea.

> I'm sick of all this risky business
>
> I want to play it safe

1. *Focus your lyric idea as clearly as you can.*

What does this say? What could it say? Is it a lyric about the dangers of dating good-looking men/women? The risk I take being with you? Why? Is "you" a flirt?

Here is a possible idea sketch:

"I thought being with you would be exciting. You are so popular and always the center of attention. I worked hard to get your attention. But now we spend time together in a whirlpool of social activity. Mostly I just feel left out. Worse, I'm afraid you don't find me exciting. Every time you say hello to someone else, I think, 'Uh-oh. This is it.' I can't stand living this way."

2. *Make a list of words that fit your idea.*

Let the list come from your idea sketch, adding any extra inspiration you have. Put them in the middle of a blank sheet of paper, number them, and enclose them in a box for easy reference later on.

Like this:

1.	scared
2.	afraid
3.	flirt
4.	attention
5.	left-out
6.	risk
7.	chance
8.	dull
9.	leave
10.	ignored
11.	gone

Find mostly *Masculine words*. Pick words with *different vowel sounds*. Your goal is to make a list of words to look up in your rhyming dictionary.

This is not a final list. As you look in the rhyming dictionary, look actively. Do not be afraid to switch, add, or take words out. You can even adjust your basic approach as you go.

3. *Look up the words on the list in your Rhyming Dictionary. Write down only rhyme words that fit with your idea.*

EXERCISE 7: LOOK UP THE WORDS IN THE LIST ABOVE IN YOUR RHYMING DICTIONARY, AND MAKE A LIST OF RHYME WORDS THAT FIT THE IDEA ON THE SHEET BELOW.

1. scared

2. afraid

3. flirt

4. attention

5. left out

6. risk

7. chance

8. dull

9. leave

10. ignored

11. gone

1. scared
2. afraid
3. flirt
4. attention
5. left-out
6. risk
7. chance
8. dull
9. leave
10. ignored
11. gone

Here is my result:

1. _scare_
   affair
   unaware
   care
   dare
   fair
   glare
   prayer
   unfair

2. _afraid_
   charade
   fade
   grade
   masquerade
   parade
   promenade

3. _flirt_
   alert
   dessert
   dirt
   hurt
   inert
   introvert
   shirt
   skirt
   unhurt

4. _attention_
   apprehension
   convention
   detention (Ident.)
   intention (Ident.)
   invention
   misapprehension
   pretension (Id.)
   suspension
   tension (Id.)

5. _left out_
   doubt
   gadabout
   knockout (Id.)
   look-out (Id.)
   scout

1.	scared
2.	afraid
3.	flirt
4.	attention
5.	left-out
6.	risk
7.	chance
8.	dull
9.	leave
10.	ignored
11.	gone

6. _risk_
   disc. . .
   (oops!)

7. _chance_
   advance
   circumstance
   dance (cliché?)
   lance
   petulance
   radiance

8. _dull_
   lull
   miracle
   numskull
   spectacle

9. _leave_
   believe (Id.)
   deceive
   grieve
   ho-heave
   sleeve

10. _ignored_
    adored
    bored
    deplored
    explored
    floored
    gored
    restored
    scored
    outscored
    sword

11. _gone_
    chiffon
    con
    ex-con
    echelon
    hangers-on
    paragon
    put upon
    dying swan

There is plenty of raw material now. A few comments on my search:

1. I left out Transitive Verbs, including "desert," since I know they are awkward in the rhyming position.
2. I left out the clichés "romance" and "trance." Did you?
3. I changed "scared" to "scare" because it had better rhymes. "Scare" is usually Transitive Verb, though it could be used as a noun. It might not me much use itself, but I like the rhyme list it generates.
4. The only chance "risk" has is to "slip a disc." I can't think of a good use for "compact disk."
5. "Ignored" didn't appear under "ORD," where I thought it should. But at the end of the column I saw "adored, etc." which referred me to "OR." The reference means to look at the "OR" column and add "d" whenever you can. The book uses this shorthand to avoid unnecessary duplication. So I went to the "OR" column and added "D." I like the list.
6. I left "safe" and "business" out of the list. If I had been starting from scratch, I would have tried them, but then eliminated them because they don't yield many rhymes.

The purpose of all this preliminary work is to *put you in charted territory* when you start writing.

EXERCISE 8: Using your WORKSHEET (OR MINE), WRITE TWO SECTIONS (MAYBE A VERSE AND A CHORUS). YOU CAN COME UP WITH YOUR OWN TITLE, OR USE "RISKY BUSINESS." (IF YOU USE MY TITLE, BE SURE NOT TO PUT IT IN A RHYMING POSITION.

EXERCISE 9: MAKE UP A WORKSHEET ON "LAST NIGHT'S LOVE." START WITH AN IDEA SKETCH. MAKE IT A HABIT TO INCLUDE EACH IMPORTANT WORD FROM THE TITLE IN YOUR LIST.

Idea sketch:

1. last

2. night

1.	last
2.	night
3.	love
4.	
5.	
6.	
7.	
8.	
9.	
10.	

3. love

Making a WORKSHEET is a great way to keep from boxing yourself into a corner. It takes time, but it also saves time. More important, it raises quality and guarantees that your rhyming position will communicate ideas effectively.

But even when you are armed with a good rhyming dictionary and have mastered making a WORKSHEET, the sad fact is that English is a "rhyme-poor" language. Why?

English does not use the endings of words in any systematic way. In other languages, like Italian, French, and Spanish, the ends of words are used for grammatical purposes: they tell you

1. whether a word is a noun, verb, adjective, etc.;
2. if the word is singular or plural;
3. how the word is being used — object of a preposition, direct object, subject, etc.;
4. how to categorize words according to gender.

English does none of these things except in two minor cases: the "ing" ending for gerunds and participles, and the "ly" ending for many adverbs.

When languages use endings in a systematic way, they limit the ways words can end, increasing rhyme possibilities. Since English does not limit the number of ways its words can end, there are fewer rhymes available. This makes it harder to use your HOT SPOTS effectively.

WORKSHEETS are very important, but, especially because of the over-use of many existing English rhymes (clichés), the options in English are severely limited. Fortunately, there are ways to improve your chances of finding effective rhymes in English even more.

CHAPTER FOUR
FAMILY FRIENDS

EXPANDING RHYME POSSIBILITIES

The writers who wrote the standards got all the good rhymes. Now they (from the grave) and their descendants (from Broadway) cajole us: "We use Perfect Rhyme. You should too." Why do they remind me of my grandfather reminiscing about his courageous thirty-mile walks through icicle storms to school? Wasn't that why his generation was so obsessive about perfecting car heaters in the first place? I have to work hard enough just to say what I mean in fresh and interesting ways. Do I have to find new uses for dead horse meat too?

It's about time to make some sense out of "Imperfect Rhymes."

First, do not be seduced by the word "perfect." It does not mean "better," it only means that

1. The syllables' *vowel sounds* are the same,
2. The sounds *after* the vowels (if any) are the same,
3. The sounds *before* the vowels are different.

Our noble forerunners, defenders of the purity of "Perfect Rhyme," too often leave us a hard choice: we are either stuck with cliché rhymes, or we have to settle for the leftovers they had the good sense not to use when they had the chance; pairings so improbable that to use them, we end up squeezing meaning around rhymes like contortionists in phone booths. You may feel like superman, but you only end up getting bent.

You will find Imperfect Rhymes very useful, and maybe even better than Perfect Rhymes for some things.

A. Imperfect rhymes give you more choices, helping you use your rhyme positions more effectively.
B. Imperfect rhymes can help you manage your structures.

The important question is whether Imperfect Rhymes will really work in a lyric. Look at a few random examples. Say them aloud.

home/alone crash/half free/bleed tide/life

Maybe yes, maybe no. Especially "tide/life." The good news is that, in a lyric, you never *say* these syllables. You would only *say* them in poetry.

Remember that lyrics are *sung*, not read or spoken. When you sing a syllable, *you hold out the vowel.* Since the vowels are exaggerated, they are much more "there" in lyrics than in poetry or prose.

Since rhyme is essentially a vowel connection, exaggerating vowels makes it possible, at least sometimes, to use Imperfect Rhymes instead of Perfect Rhymes.

Look at them again. This time, *sing them.*

home/alone crash/half free/bleed tide/life

You can hear how much better they connect when you sing them. The vowels really hook into each other. The differences between the consonants are not nearly as noticeable.

The way a lyric exaggerates vowel connections should make it possible, at least in some cases, for you to use Imperfect Rhymes instead of Perfect Rhymes.

There are different kinds of Imperfect Rhymes. Some are very close to Perfect Rhyme, so it will be easy for you to use them to substitute for Perfect Rhyme. Others are not very close, and will not work as well as substitutes. You may still be able to use them, but you should clearly understand what you are doing and why.

I will start with PERFECT RHYME SUBSTITUTES and then move progressively further away.

PERFECT RHYME SUBSTITUTES

There are two Imperfect Rhyme Types that you can normally use in place of Perfect Rhyme:

1. FAMILY RHYME
2. ADDITIVE/SUBTRACTIVE RHYME

Both types will give you many more choices than Perfect Rhyme. They will help you use rhyming positions effectively. By combining them with Perfect Rhyme in a WORKSHEET, you can make rhyme your friend forever.

Family Rhyme

1. The syllables' vowel sounds are the same,
2. The sounds after the vowels are *phonetic relatives,*
3. The sounds before the vowels are different.

Family Rhymes are the same as Perfect Rhymes except for one thing. The consonants after the vowel are not the same, they are phonetic relatives. That is why I call them "Family" Rhymes.

When two consonants are phonetically related, we can trade one in for the other and get a Family Rhyme.

Say you are looking for a rhyme for

safe

Look at the consonant after the long *a* vowel:, "f." If you knew what consonants are phonetically related to "f," you could look in your rhyming dictionary under

Ā + *consonant phonetically related to "f"*

Presto! You would have a Family Rhyme. All you need to know is how to find phonetic relatives. I'll show you.

(Your job as a lyricist is to come up with ideas; to create sections, language rhythms, and sounds. If you want to make sounds work for you, you should try your best to understand them.)

Vowels are tone generators. Consonants cluster around them. Consonants can relate to each other because they produce sounds either by

a. using the same technique,
b. using the same physical positions,
c. using (or not using) the vocal cords.

When two consonants share any of these relationships, they are phonetically related.

When two consonants are phonetically related, we can substitute one for the other in the syllable after the vowel and get a Family Rhyme.

That is how you find Family Rhymes.

Phonetic Relationships

The most general phonetic relationship is between consonants that use the same technique to produce sound. Consonants divide into three groups according to technique:

1. Plosives
2. Fricatives
3. Nasals

Plosives

The word "Plosive" means just what you think; a little explosion of air. As you talk (or sing), the air column coming out of your mouth is stopped. Pressure builds up and then explodes to make the consonant sound.

Go through the alphabet. Don't say the *names* of the letters, just use the *sounds* they make in words.

Right. The first one is "b." You build up pressure by stopping your air column with your lips, then exploding.

Next comes "d." Touch the tip of your tongue to your hard palate to stop your air column and build pressure. Then explode.

Now "g." The middle of your tongue touches your soft palate, stops your air column, builds pressure, then explodes. Just a little explosion. It happens very fast.

There are three more: "k," "p," and "t."

Do these positions feel familiar? They should. They are the same as "b," "d," and "g." In fact, b = p, d = t, and g = k. Then how are they different?

Try "p." It feels like you are spitting air. Now make a sound with your vocal cords while you are doing it. The result sounds exactly like a "b," in fact, it is a "b." They are both Plosives, they both use the same physical positions, but "b" is VOICED and "p" is UNVOICED.

Look again at the ways phonetic relationships are formed: by producing sounds

a. using the same technique,
b. using the same physical positions,
c. using (or not using) the vocal cords.

All six plosives use the same exploding technique. They all fit the first criterion.

a. using the same technique

> b, d, g, p, t, k

Within the Plosive family, there are further relationships.

b. using the same physical positions,

> b = p d = t g = k

Call this extra relationship "*Partners.*" Partners use the same physical positions.

c. using (or not using) the vocal cords,

> b = d = g p = t = k

Call this extra relationship "*Companions.*" Companions have the same voicing characteristic.

When two consonants belong to the same Family, *plus* have an extra relationship (either Partners or Companions), they are better Perfect Rhyme Substitutes.

We can summarize these results with a table:

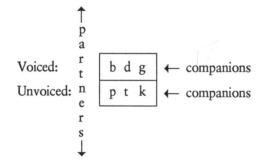

Here are the practical results: if a syllable ends in a plosive, there are FIVE more places to look for rhymes in addition to Perfect Rhyme. There is even an order to look in.

Say you want to find a rhyme for "rut":

First, look at Perfect Rhymes. The vowel sound is short ŭ. These seem like the possibilities:

> rut
> cut
> glut
> gut
> hut
> shut

It is time to try Family Rhymes.

"T" (the consonant ending "rut") is an Unvoiced Plosive. Partners are the closest relationship for plosives. Check the table. "T's" partner is "d." Now find the same vowel sound (the short ŭ) ending with "d" in the rhyming dictionary. Under short "ŭ + d" you find, among other entries,

_ud_
blood
flood
mud
stud (?)
thud

These are nice possibilities, especially "flood" and "mud."

Now, move back to "t's" COMPANIONS, "k" and "p."

_uk_
buck
duck
luck
muck
stuck
truck

This is getting better. All of these are nice.

_up_
hard-up
up
make-up (?)

"Make-up" suggests that the relationship is in a rut, we have a fight, etc.

We have now finished Plosives with closer relationships to "t." Finally, look at "b" and "g," which share *only* that they are formed the same way — by exploding.

_ub_
club
hub
pub
scrub
tub

These do not sound quite the same. Sing them. "Ruuuuuut. Scruuuuuub." Not so bad. Good, in fact. Some good ones here too.

_ug_
bug
jug
lug
plug
shrug
snug
tug

These are some of the best yet. You have now completed a search for Family Rhyme, based on simple phonetic reasoning. If you stay with Perfect Rhyme, this is what you have:

rut

cut

glut

gut

hut

shut

Family Rhymes deliver these additional choices:

_ud_	_uk_	_up_	_ub_	_ug_
blood	buck	hard-up	lub	bug
flood	duck	up	hub	jug
mud	luck	make-up	pub	lug
thud	muck		scrub	plug
	stuck		tub	shrug
	truck			snug
				tug

Roughly, Family Rhyme offers about five times more choices. Not all great, but then the five choices offered by Perfect Rhyme could be better too. Here are the ones I would actually consider using:

rut
shut

_ud_	_uk_	_up_	_ub_	_ug_
flood	luck	up	pub	shrug
mud	muck		scrub	snug
	stuck		tub	tug
	truck			

EXERCISE 10: USING YOUR RHYMING DICTIONARY, FIND RELATED PERFECT RHYMES FOR "LEAGUE." THEN FIND FAMILY RHYMES, WORKING FROM CLOSER PHONETIC RELATIONSHIPS TO THOSE FURTHER AWAY.

Gee

Be careful with "g." You make the sound near the back of your mouth (by touching the middle of your tongue to your soft palate). Your mouth changes the sounds of most short vowels as you prepare to make the "g" sound. "G" will not give you a Perfect Rhyme Substitute in these cases:

short ă as in "hag." It does not sound like "hat."
short ĕ as in "egg." It does not sound like "ebb."
short ĭ as in "big." It does not sound like "bid."
short ŏ as in "log." It does not sound like "lob."
(But you may use ô as in "fraud," "hawk," "fought" to extend your options when you start with "log.")

You can use "g" with these vowels:

long ā as in "vague." long ē as in "league."
long ō as in "vogue." long ū as in "fugue" (the only one).
short ŭ as in "rug"

As a rule of thumb: "Long — yes. Short — no." You do not have to memorize this list. Your ear will tell you fast enough. Never stop listening.

Fricatives

You make "Fricatives" by slowing the air flow out of your mouth enough to cause friction; a little like a leaking air hose. Stop reading and go through the alphabet to find them. Again, don't say the letters' *names*. Make the *sounds* they make in words.

The first one in the alphabet is "f." You close your top teeth against your bottom lip enough to restrict the air flow. Use your vocal cords and you get "v."

Next you get "j." It has a slight explosion right at the beginning, but it is still mainly a Fricative. The front of your tongue rises toward your hard palate until it restricts the air flow, causing friction and sound. "J" is voiced. Without your vocal cords it is "ch."

You probably got "s," the air hose sound, next. Your tongue rises to your hard palate again but with a flatter and more forward motion than "j." "S" is unvoiced. With your vocal cords it becomes "z."

Most likely you missed "sh." It is the "ch" sound without the little explosion at the beginning. When you use your vocal cords it becomes a "zh" sound, as in "beige."

The last one, which you may have also missed, is "th." Except for "f," it is the most forward Fricative. You trap air between your tongue and top teeth. It is unvoiced, like the last sound of "faith." If you use your vocal cords, it is the sound at the end of "baTHe." Use capital letters to mark the voiced TH and small letters for unvoiced th.

Here is the expanded table:

	partners ↑								
Voiced:		b	d	g	v	TH	z	zh	j	← companions
Unvoiced:		p	t	k	f	th	s	sh	ch	← companions

When using Fricatives, COMPANIONS are closer than PARTNERS. The opposite was true for Plosives. Fricatives take longer to say than Plosives, so you hear the unvoiced or voiced sound more clearly.

Also, Fricatives are closer together in your mouth than plosives. *All* the Fricatives come from the area in your mouth *between* "b" and "d."

For Fricative Family Rhymes, go to all the COMPANIONS *before* you cross over. Then to the PARTNER, then all its COMPANIONS.

Whether you are working with Fricatives or Plosives, COMPANIONS start closest and move outward. If you are working with "sh," you would go from "ch" to "s," "th" and finally, "f." Try it. Start with Perfect Rhymes for "safe." "F" is an Unvoiced Fricative.

safe
waif

Ugh! See if we can get any help from Family Rhymes.

ath
faith

Not much. Next is "s."

as
case
ace
breathing-space
chase
commonplace
disgrace
embrace
face
grace
lace
race
space

Much better. There are some nice choices here. I didn't pick "erase" or "trace" because they are Transitive Verbs. They need to be completed by a Direct Object:

erase *my heart*

trace *your feelings*

They would be awkward in the rhyming position.

Words like "chase" and "embrace," even though as verbs they are Transitive, can be nouns, so there is no problem picking them.

There is nothing worthwhile under "ash" or "ach." Time to cross the line to "f's" PARTNER, "v."

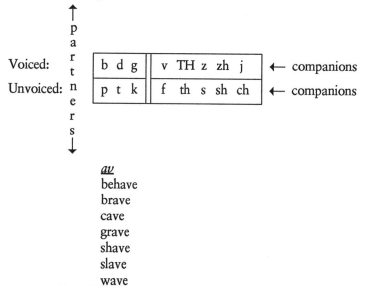

av
behave
brave
cave
grave
shave
slave
wave

Again, I left out "crave" and "forgave" because they are Transitive Verbs. I left out "gave" because it is bland.

aTH
bathe

Fat chance.

az
blaze
craze
daze
haze
maze
phrase
paraphrase
praise

The nice thing about a cliché word like "daze" is that it may sound fresh again away from its usual connection to "haze." That is another strength of Family Rhyme. They surprise you. They do not make the usual connections.

aj
age
cage
page
rage
stage

Words like "lineage" are interesting. The secondary stress on the last syllable is a different sound. "Lineage" will not work as a Family Rhyme for "safe." But then, it will not work with "age" either.

We got good results with Family Rhymes for "safe."

as	*av*	*az*	*aj*
case	behave	blaze	age
ace	brave	craze	cage
breathing-space	cave	daze	page
chase	grave	haze	rage
commonplace	shave	phrase	stage
disgrace	slave	paraphrase	
embrace	wave	praise	
face			
grace		*aTH*	
lace		bathe	
race			
resting-place		*ath*	
space		faith	

Feminine searches are also effective. Here is a quick one:

travel
bashful
dazzle
wrathful
glass full (mosaic)
satchel
fragile

Some Fricatives offer few results, while with others, results come cascading in. Usually you at least quadruple your choices with Fricative Family Rhymes.

EXERCISE 11: USING YOUR RHYMING DICTIONARY, FIND RELATED PERFECT RHYMES FOR "TOUCH." THEN FIND FAMILY RHYMES, WORKING FROM CLOSER PHONETIC RELATIONSHIPS TO THOSE FURTHER AWAY.

Nasals

The word "Nasals" means what you think it means. When you say a nasal, you make all the sound come out of your nose. Stop reading and find them.

Right. "M" and "n." You missed "ng" as in "sing."

For "m" your lips are closed, so your mouth acts as an extra resonating chamber.

For "n" you raise the tip of your tongue to your hard palate to stop the sound from coming out of your mouth. Only half of your mouth is used as an extra resonating chamber.

For "ng" you raise the middle of your tongue to your soft palate and prevent your mouth from being used as a sound resonating chamber at all.

Nasal mouth positions are like the Plosive mouth positions, except that when you block the air, you send sound out of your nose rather than letting the pressure build to an explosion.

What if you have a cold and are not able to get air out of your nose? Plug your nose and say,

"My mommy misses me."

"M" turns into "b." Plug your nose and say,

"No one notices Nanna."

"N" becomes "d." Plug your nose and say,

"I sing songs that ring wrong."

"Ng" turns into "g." Too bad you can't use these related Plosives as rhyme substitutes. All of the Nasals are voiced. They only have COMPANIONS.

Voiced: | m n ng | ← companions

Here is the final table for Family Rhymes:

	PLOSIVES	FRICATIVES	NASALS	
Voiced:	b d g	v TH z zh j	m n ng	← companions
Unvoiced:	p t k	f th s sh ch		← companions

↑ p a r t n e r s ↓

Look up Perfect Rhymes for "home."

> *home*
> catacomb
> comb
> hippodrome
> honey-comb
> Nome

I resisted "roam" because it is an expected cliché (though it might sound fresh rhymed with "alone"). Now find Family Rhymes. Not much mystery where to look:

> *on*
> blown
> bone
> chaperone
> cornerstone
> gramaphone
> grown (cliché?)
> throne
> undertone
> zone

There is plenty to choose from here, depending on what you are writing about. No need to pick commonplaces like "alone" "phone" or "own" with all this interesting material.

Oddly, "alone" is a cliché rhyme with "home." Even some sticklers for Perfect Rhyme use it, maybe without noticing.

You saw that "ng" does not work with long ō. In fact, "ng" NEVER works with long vowels and works with only two of the short ones:

> short ŏ as in "gone/wrong"
> short ŭ as in "fun/rung"

Mostly, "ng" is no help. But when it DOES help, it helps a lot.

EXERCISE 12: USING YOUR RHYMING DICTIONARY, FIND RELATED PERFECT RHYMES FOR "WON." THEN FIND FAMILY RHYMES, WORKING FROM CLOSER PHONETIC RELATIONSHIPS TO THOSE FURTHER AWAY.

Feminine Family Rhymes

So far we have worked mostly with masculine rhymes. But Family Rhymes are just as easy to find for Feminine Rhymes, and just as valuable. Remember to work with the stressed syllables in Feminine Rhymes. Treat them as if they were the only syllable there. If you want to rhyme

> lonely

just look at the stressed syllable

> lone.

The consonant after the vowel, "n," is a Nasal. The substitute for "n" is "m." So look under "ŎM-li" in the Feminine section. You will find

> homely.

Not a bad connection either.

You can find Feminine Family Rhymes anytime the stressed syllable ends in a Plosive, Fricative, or Nasal. Just use the table as usual, then look in section two (the feminine section) of the rhyming dictionary. To rhyme

> table

work with the accented syllable, "tab."

"B" is a Voiced Plosive. First use "b's" partner, "p." Under "ĀP'l" in the feminine section of the rhyming dictionary you find

> maple.

Move next to "d," and under "ĀD'l" you can find

> ladle.

And so on. The pickings are pretty slim in the feminine section, so any additional possibilities are like gold.

Sometimes you will be able to work with the feminine word's stressed syllable in the masculine section (especially when the unstressed syllable rhymes with pronoun). You might get

> homely/phone me
> believer/please her

As you can see, mosaic rhymes work just as well as Family Rhymes.

(A neat trick: if the tone of your lyric is informal, you might try dropping the "g" on Feminine "ing" words, like "sailing." Then you can create a Mosaic Rhyme with "him":

> sailin'
> tail him

This trick works especially well in Country, where "g" is dropped almost as a matter of principle.)

Since there is so much identity after the rhyme at the stressed vowel (another whole syllable in fact), Feminine Family Rhymes are strong substitutes for Perfect Rhymes.

EXERCISE 13: USING YOUR RHYMING DICTIONARY, FIND PERFECT RHYMES FOR "TAKING."
THEN FIND FAMILY RHYMES, WORKING FROM THE CLOSEST RELATIONSHIPS TO THOSE FURTHER
AWAY.

Syllables Ending in More Than One Consonant

You can also use Family Rhyme techniques when a syllable ends in more than one consonant.
Just look up Family Rhymes for each consonant in turn. Or, find substitutes for both. Try

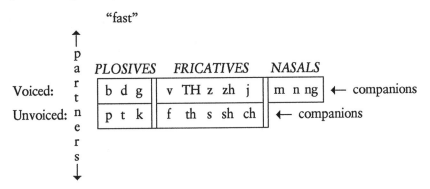

If the first consonant is Unvoiced, the following one will be Unvoiced too. In

ashed,

the "ed" sounds like "t." Just look under "ăsh + t":

ashed
bashed
cashed
clashed
crashed
dashed
flashed
lashed
splashed
thrashed
unlashed

A pretty amazing list. Now "f + t":

aft   ăf + ed
craft
draft
raft
shaft
autographed
gaffed
laughed
photographed

Good results. Now "ch + t":

ach + ed
attached
dispatched
matched
scratched
snatched

Now look for Family relations of "t" in "fast," keeping "s":

asp
clasp
gasp
grasp
rasp

Next, to

ask
flask
mask
task

When you move to the Voiced Fricatives, the "t" sound becomes Voiced as "d."

azd
jazzed
razzed

For "fast," the Voiced Fricatives turn out to be little help. Not that you needed any. Whenever a syllable has two or more consonants after the vowel, the choices stack up pretty fast.

EXERCISE 14: USING YOUR RHYMING DICTIONARY, FIND RELATED PERFECT RHYMES FOR "DRUNK." THEN FIND FAMILY RHYMES, WORKING FROM CLOSER PHONETIC RELATIONSHIPS TO THOSE FURTHER AWAY.

L and R

You will find the above techniques especially useful when one of the consonants after the vowel is "l" or "r." Neither "l" nor "r" has a useful Family substitute. But when either one appears with a consonant that has Family relationships, your rhyme search is easier. Look up Perfect Rhymes for

> *hurt*
> alert
> curt
> dirt
> flirt
> inert
> skirt

Many Perfect Rhymes for "hurt" are Transitive Verbs. That limits your options. Now look for Family Rhymes. "T" is an Unvoiced Plosive.

> *urd*
> absurd
> gallows-bird
> stirred
> word

(Good news! You can use the past-tense verbs of "ur.")

> blurred
> deterred
> preferred
> purred
> slurred

Move to COMPANIONS.

> *urp*
> burp
> twerp

> *urk*
> jerk
> quirk
> smirk
> dirty-work

And to the other Voiced Plosives:

> *urb*   *urg*
> curb   iceberg
> suburb

EXERCISE 15: Find related Perfect Rhymes for "heart." Then find Family Rhymes, substituting for "t," working from closer phonetic relationships to those further away.

Now try "l." Find Perfect Rhymes for

> *help*
> kelp ?
> oops!
>
> *eld*
> unparalleled
> weld

(Good news! You can use the past-tense verbs of "el.")

> compelled
> propelled
> quelled
> rebelled
> shelled

Move to COMPANIONS.

> *elt*
> elt
> felt
> heart-felt
> melt

Nothing anywhere else. But the expansion is not bad, considering you had nothing at all for "help."

EXERCISE 16: FIND RELATED PERFECT RHYMES FOR "YOURSELF." THEN FIND FAMILY RHYMES, SUBSTITUTING "F," WORKING FROM CLOSER PHONETIC RELATIONSHIPS TO THOSE FURTHER AWAY.

Now that you have gotten to know Family Rhyme you should be feeling better. Finding rhymes is not so hard after all.

Family Rhymes give you legitimate substitutes for Perfect Rhymes. They have immediate benefits:

1. They give you more choices, helping you to use your rhyming positions more effectively.
2. They help you avoid the cliché rhymes so common in Perfect Rhyme.
3. And, as you will see soon, they help you control structure.

Again, Family Rhyme is a practical possibility because of the phonetic relationships between consonants that follow the vowel sounds. Since lyrics are *sung*, vowel sounds are promoted and consonant sounds are demoted. If you take the time to sing the Family Rhymes, they will not trouble your sensibilities. They will sound like "real rhymes!"

CHAPTER FIVE
FRIENDLY RELATIVES

ADDITIVE/SUBTRACTIVE RHYME

Sometimes you need to look further than Family Rhyme. There are two clear cases:

1. When words end in vowels.
2. When your Family Rhyme search has not given you acceptable choices.

WORDS ENDING IN VOWELS

Family Rhymes depend on consonants *after* the syllables' stressed vowels. When there are *no* consonants after the vowels, Family Rhymes are clearly impossible. You will find many words that end in vowels. They are called "Open Vowels." Except for the ä in "father," they are all long vowels:

Ā	in	"play"
ä	in	"father"
Ē	in	"free"
Ī	in	"die"
Ō	in	"go"
Ū	in	"few" and "shampoo"

For Masculine rhymes, Open Vowels are listed at the beginning of each vowel section.

Feminine Rhymes list Open Vowels alphabetically according to the consonant at the beginning of the unstressed syllable.

data	=	Ā + ta
viva	=	Ē + va
riot	=	Ī + ot
heroic	=	Ō + ik
stupid	=	Ū + pid

For decades lyricists have preferred rhymes that end with vowels. Rupert Holmes says that he likes to hold the vowel at the end of the phrase without "tailing off" into a consonant. It is a good idea. The problem is that "Open Rhymes" have been used so often, that most of them are cliché.

One of the nice things about Perfect Rhyme substitutes is they bypass the old clichés.

Whenever your stressed syllable ends in a vowel, *you can find additional rhymes by adding consonants.* The clearest case is the simple plural.

> free
> trees

Sometimes you need to use a plural word, yet its rhyme is singular. Do it. There is no need to turn somersaults trying to make the singular into a plural. The rhyme works just fine. Call it ADDITIVE RHYME.

Simple plurals aren't the only way to get Additive Rhyme. If

> free
> trees

works, than so does

> free
> peace
> police
> release.

You can get rhymes that connect ideas and create action.

Very simply, Additive Rhyme *adds* a consonant(s) after the vowel sound. More precisely, in Additive Rhymes

1. The syllables' vowel sounds are the same
2. *One of the syllables has an extra consonant(s).*
3. The sounds BEFORE the vowels are different.

If you just go by the definition, it looks easy. But be careful. According to the definition ANY syllable with the same vowel sound as "free" will technically be an Additive Rhyme, even

> free
> shields.

Though you can still hear the common vowel sound, the relationship is not strong enough to *substitute* for Perfect Rhyme. There is too much difference in sound.

How much is too much? Tough question. It depends on how noticeable the consonants are, and maybe on the length of the syllables' note. Here are some guidelines:

—In general, *the less you add,* the better the rhyme works as a Perfect Rhyme Substitute.

—Consonants that take the *shortest time to say* are the least noticeable. So start with plosives.

—*Voiced Plosives* are less noticeable than Unvoiced Plosives.

—The *further forward* the sound is in your mouth, the less noticeable it is.

—Avoid adding Nasals. Other than "l" and "r," they are the most noticeable consonants.

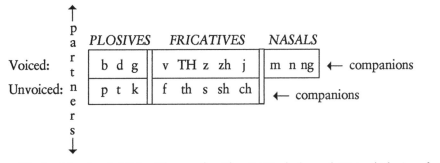

Try looking for Additive Rhymes for "free." Work through Voiced Plosives from front to back, then go to Unvoiced Plosives, front to back.

> *free*
>
> *+b*
> oops!
>
> *+d*
> bleed
> greed
> speed
> seed. . . etc.
>
> *+p*
> deep
> asleep
> cheap
> weep
>
> *+t*
> bitter-sweet
> deceit
> defeat (noun)
> elite

+*k*
bleak
speak
weak

If these do not deliver what you need, go to the next least noticeable sound, Unvoiced Fricatives, front to back:

+*f*
belief
relief
thief

+*s*
peace
police
release . . . etc.

NEVER STOP LISTENING. If your ear says a sound is wrong, find another rhyme. TRUST YOUR EARS. (But be sure to sing your rhymes when you check.)

EXERCISE 17: USING YOUR RHYMING DICTIONARY, FIND RELATED PERFECT RHYMES FOR "GOODBYE." THEN FIND ADDITIVE RHYMES, STARTING WITH UNVOICED PLOSIVES, MOVING TO VOICED PLOSIVES, THEN TO UNVOICED FRICATIVES.

SYLLABLES WITH CONSONANT ENDINGS

Additive Rhyme also works when each syllable ends with the same consonant(s). You simply add another one.

> erase
> pa*ste*

Work the same way you did in the last exercise. Start with Unvoiced Plosives and continue from there.

Remember this?

"... as
case
ace
breathing-space ...

   Much better. There are some nice choices here. I did not pick "erase" or "trace" because they are Transitive Verbs. They need to be completed by a Direct Object.

erase *my heart*
trace *your feelings* ..."

The old "Transitive Verb Bugaboo." But now you can solve the problem by adding "ed" to change the verb from Active to Passive:

> *as*
> case
> ace
> breathing-space
> erased
> traced

Terrific. You have just regained all the Transitive Verbs you had to bypass earlier. There IS a price: Active Verbs are stronger than Passive Verbs. But at least you get to use them without making your phrases sound unnatural. Instead of this clumsy relic,

> You say you need some breathing-space
>
> As *if my heart you could erase* (Ick)

you get this:

> You say you need some breathing-space
>
> As if my heart could be erased

An added attraction is that the unvoiced "s" makes the final "d" turn into an Unvoiced "t" sound.

The technique is especially nice for syllables that end in "r" or "l." The sound of both consonants is so strong that, when they are combined with a vowel, whatever comes after them will hardly be noticeable.

> *scar*
> heart
> dark
> tarred
> guard
> charge
> hearth

Or this:

> *Jezebel*
> unparalleled
> help
> knelt
> svelte
> wealth

These work very well, better than many Additive Rhymes, because "l" and "r" carry so much weight. You might even get away with additional consonants.

> sta*r*
> ar*ms*

Maybe even this far:

> war
> endor*sed*

Again, sing them. Trust your ears.

EXERCISE 18: USING YOUR RHYMING DICTIONARY, FIND RELATED PERFECT RHYMES FOR "STONE." THEN FIND ADDITIVE RHYMES, STARTING WITH UNVOICED PLOSIVES, MOVING TO VOICED PLOSIVES, THEN TO UNVOICED FRICATIVES.

FAMILY ADDITIVES

Besides using Additive Rhymes to rescue Transitive Verbs and increase choices for "l" and "r," you can extend this technique. Anytime you are searching for Family Rhyme, stay alert for Additive Rhymes along the way. You could run into pairs like these:

conde*mn*	love	tri*p*	a*ch*e
defe*nd*	bluffs	ris*k*	sai*nt*

You cannot find the last two pairs alphabetically because the extra consonant comes *before* the Family consonant. Keep your eyes open for them. They will drop out of the sky. Stars fall all the time. If you are watching for them, you will see some.

EXERCISE 19: USING YOUR RHYMING DICTIONARY, FIND RELATED PERFECT RHYMES FOR "HUSH." NEXT, LOOK FOR FAMILY RHYMES. WHILE YOU ARE LOOKING, WATCH FOR FAMILY ADDITIVE RHYMES, ESPECIALLY WITH UNVOICED OR VOICED PLOSIVES. BE ON THE LOOKOUT FOR PLACES WHERE THE EXTRA CONSONANT COMES BEFORE THE FAMILY CONSONANT. (EVEN IN THE NASALS, SINCE THIS ADDITION IS INSIDE THE WORD AND IS NOT QUITE SO NOTICEABLE. YOU COULD GET SOMETHING LIKE "LUNCH," WHICH SEEMS TO WORK JUST FINE.)

SUBTRACTIVE RHYME

When a syllable ends with consonants, you can reverse your Additive Rhyme techniques and get SUBTRACTIVE RHYME. Its definition is the same. The way you get it is different.

1. The syllables' vowel sounds are the same
2. *One of the syllables has an extra consonant(s).*
3. The sounds BEFORE the vowels are different.

Start with a syllable that has two consonants:

> fast

Subtract the *least* noticeable consonant, then look up rhymes. "Ăst" minus "t" = "ăs."

> *ăs*
> class
> mass
> lass
> pass

You can try subtracting the more noticeable consonant. THEN LISTEN to the result to see if it works. In this case you could get

> *ăs*
> brat
> aristocrat

Of course, as you saw earlier, the usual Family techniques are available. Since "s" is the most noticeable sound, keep it and look in the families for "t."

>   clasp
>   ask . . .

Then try adding "t" to the Fricative families for "s." You will get words like

>   draft

Finally, try simple Family Rhymes for

> *as*
> dash
> wrath
> laugh . . .

Try them. "Fast/dash" is a lovely connection. It is NOT a cliché rhyme, and it is an acceptable Perfect Rhyme substitute.

When you work with long vowels that end in only one consonant, you can always pare down to the open vowel:

>   treat
>   free

No need to multiply examples. You understand.

EXERCISE 20: USING YOUR RHYMING DICTIONARY, FIND RELATED PERFECT RHYMES FOR "TRICKS."

tricks:

Substitute Family Rhymes for each consonant:

tricks: (substitute for "k")

tricks: (substitute for s)

Now find Subtractive Rhymes by subtracting the *weakest* consonant and looking for Perfect Rhymes for the result:

tris:

Now Family Rhymes for "tris":

Write a verse using some of your results.

Remember that these techniques work just as easily for Feminine Rhymes as they do for Masculine Rhyme. I have been using Masculine Rhyme for simplicity and clarity. (Try finding one for "simply.")

You have now been through all the rhyme types that can substitute for Perfect Rhyme. Family Rhyme and Additive/Subtractive Rhyme are easy to find. Both allow you to use your rhyming positions expressively, giving you fresh options in what has become a mine field of clichés. And finally, both retain the power over structure that is characteristic of Perfect Rhyme.

The next chapter will move further from Perfect Rhyme. The further you move from Perfect Rhyme, the less your rhyme affects structure. But as you will see, this can also be a hidden benefit.

CHAPTER SIX
KISSIN' COUSINS

So far we have worked with rhyme types that, for the most part, work like Perfect Rhyme. Because we have been careful to *minimize* the differences between the sounds after the vowels, these rhyme types are able to preserve the tension/resolution characteristics that make rhyme work.

We will now look at more remote rhyme types. They have many of the qualities that you value, plus they can do things for you that we can't get from any of our friends so far: they can suppress or at least diminish the effects on lyric structure that should result naturally from rhyme schemes. (See Chapter Four of my book, *Song Lyrics; How to Create and Manage Structire.*)

They still give you the main rhyming benefit, expressive use of the rhyming position. But they give you something extra, a more subtle control of structure, new ways to affect the MOVING and STOPPING of structures. These new techniques will be useful tools.

We will look at these rhyme types:

1. Assonance Rhymes
2. Consonance Rhymes
3. Partial Rhymes
4. Weak-syllable Rhymes

ASSONANCE RHYME

Assonance Rhyme is simple vowel rhyme. The only thing the syllables share in common is their vowel sound. More precisely, in Assonance Rhyme,

1. The syllables' vowel sounds are the same
2. The consonants after the vowel are unrelated
3. The sounds before the vowels are different.

Assonance Rhyme *always* has consonants after the vowel, but they are not phonetically related. Although the vowel connections can still heard when the syllables are sung, such different endings prevent the resolution from being complete.

Some examples:

love/hunt tide/afterlife

Sing them. You can hear their connection. The vowel sounds ring out and connect. However, they do not complete their connection; they leave it hanging.

Finding Assonance Rhymes in the rhyming dictionary is easy. Just look in all the places you wouldn't look for Perfect Rhyme, Family Rhyme, Additive Rhyme, or Subtractive Rhyme. You have to look at every column headed by the vowel you need.

This is the widest possible rhyme search, but a manageable one. An Assonance search on the word "tide" for example, involves looking in the rhyming dictionary under ALL the long ī columns. The search takes time, but the rewards are usually worth it:

tide
life
isle
climb
brine
life-line
rise
survive
revive

EXERCISE 21: USING YOUR RHYMING DICTIONARY, FIND RELATED ASSONANCE RHYMES FOR THE WORDS BELOW.

1. race _____ _____ _____ _____ _____

2. plan _____ _____ _____ _____ _____

3. French _____ _____ _____ _____ _____

4. treat _____ _____ _____ _____ _____

5. file _____ _____ _____ _____ _____

6. trip _____ _____ _____ _____ _____

7. robbed _____ _____ _____ _____ _____

8. scold _____ _____ _____ _____ _____

9. fuse _____ _____ _____ _____ _____

10. luck _____ _____ _____ _____ _____

FEMININE ASSONANCE RHYME

Feminine Assonance Rhymes are usually stronger than Masculine Assonance Rhymes because of the extended resolution of the unstressed syllables. For Assonance Rhyme, the extended resolution is a real benefit. It makes a much stronger rhyming connection than Masculine Assonance Rhyme. So solid, in fact, that it is usually a good Perfect Rhyme Substitute.

Try this:

> lonely

You already know the available Family Rhymes from the nasals. You can now look for Plosives and Fricatives. Just go through the Feminine long ō section and look for the unstressed syllables ending in "i" (the Feminine section's notation for unaccented long ē), "li," and even "ing." Pick up whatever else falls from the sky along the way.

lonely

adobe	disrobing
approaching	probing
reproaching	toady
foreboding	trophy
solely	snowy (subtractive)
smokey	blowing (subtractive)
yogi	pokey
coldly	boldly
stogie	holy ⎤
dopey	lowly ⎬ (subtractive)
coyote	slowly ⎦
imposing	consoling . . . etc.
hoping	alimony (subtractive)
ghostly	voting
anchovy	nosy (subtractive)

Sing them. Many will be fine as Perfect Rhyme substitutes. Others will not. The latter will have to stay as Assonance Rhymes.

You can still find Mosaics. One way is to use Masculine Transitive Verbs plus the pronoun "me," as in

lonely
hold me
close me

EXERCISE 22: USING YOUR RHYMING DICTIONARY, FIND RELATED FEMININE ASSONANCE RHYMES FOR "save me."

EFFECTS ON STRUCTURE

Look at a typical "a b a b" rhyme scheme close with Perfect Rhyme:

swim	a
tide	b
skim	a
ride	b

It stays a little open if you use Assonance Rhyme in the resolving position:

swim	a
tide	b
skim	a
rise	b

Both examples *sound* like an "a b a b" rhyme structure, but the ending in the second one doesn't give the resounding THWACK that you feel in the first one. It seems to hang open a little, *but it makes the connection.*

This feeling of partial openness is what makes some people condemn Assonance Rhyme with the pejorative "false rhyme." But this is the very feature that makes it such a handy tool. The trick, of course, is to know what you are using, and when and how to use it.

Look again at this rhyme scheme:

a	—	1
b	—	2
a	—	3
b	—	4

In the "a b a b" rhyme structure, Assonance Rhyme modifies the closure slightly when it appears in the resolving position (2 and 4). When it appears in 1 and 3, it modifies the forward push the structure gives at 3. Instead of

swim	1
tide	2
skim →	3

forcing motion forward to a match with "tide," an Assonance Rhyme, like

swim	1
tide	2
drift . . .	3

tends to relax the push forward.

The whole structure relaxes if we use Assonance Rhyme in both the pushing position (3) and the resolving position (4):

swim	1
tide	2
drift	3
rise	4

The structure neither pushes forward firmly nor closes solidly. Its motion, in this case, could be appropriate for the ideas it uses — a little like a lazy float in Acapulco Bay. The sonic connections are made; the rhyming position still draws your ear, but the structural effects are no longer so crisp and definite.

Look at another rhyme scheme. This one has a built in acceleration:

swim	a
tide	b
drown	c
down	c
night	b

The acceleration seems appropriate in this tale of tragedy. But with a happier ending, damping the acceleration might be useful:

swim	a
tide	b
drown	c
roused	c
night	b

This feels a little like slow motion; like waking up from a bad dream. The sonic connection is made, but the effect is not nearly as crisp as it was with Perfect Rhyme. That seems to be an advantage in this case.

Assonance Rhyme is a great tool for connecting ideas. The relative looseness of rhyme connection, damping rhyme's effect on structure, can be handled in one of two ways:

1. "Let it happen; in this particular point in my lyric I can stand the rhyme's effect on structure being somewhat suppressed."
2. "I love the *content* of this Assonance Rhyme, but I still need the effect of Perfect Rhyme in the structure. Therefore I will make a *musical commitment*: I will extend the note at this point, to emphasize the vowel connection even more. Maybe I can use something in the melody or the chords to make up for the rhyme's openness. (Listen to Stevie Nicks sing the word "life" to connect it with "tide" in "Landslide.")

The beauty of Assonance Rhyme is its versatility. You can use it when you want better words in your rhyming position. You can control structural motion more precisely, and use your rhyming positions more effectively by adding Assonance Rhyme to your circle of friends. The only question is when and how to use it. If you stay alert to the possibilities, they are usually easy to see. A little like falling stars.

CONSONANCE RHYME

From Birth to Death

For Consonance Rhyme,

1. The syllables' *vowel sounds are DIFFERENT.*
2. The consonants after the vowel are the SAME.

Look:

save	sin	word
leave	sun	card

Consonance rhyme creates tension/resolution by making the vowel sounds different, using the final consonants as resolution. The final consonants must be the same. Family relationships do not count here. The beginning consonants can be either different or the same, it doesn't matter. Thus "thad/thud" is just as effective as "cave/give."

You often find Consonance Rhymes in poetry. Since poetry is read or spoken rather than sung, it does not exaggerate vowel sounds like the lyric does. In a poem, the vowels and consonants are much more equal partners.

In a lyric, connections between consonant sounds must be very strong to even hear them.

In order, these Consonance Rhymes are the most likely to be useful:

1. *Feminine Consonance Rhymes*. As usual, the identity or rhyme of the unstressed syllable gives you extra resolution, making Feminine Consonance Rhyme stronger than its Masculine counterpart.

cra*mming*	ru*bber*
tee*ming*	fi*bber*

2. *Masculine Consonance Rhymes containing "r" or "l."* Since the sound of these consonants is so strong, they are very hard to miss.

sca*r*e	pu*ll*	sna*rl*
fea*r*	fa*ll*	cu*rl*

3. *Masculine* Consonance rhymes *ending in multiple consonants*. There is a lot of common sound to hear:

ra*nch*	fa*st*	cry*pt*
ly*nch*	re*st*	sle*pt*

4. *Masculine* Consonance rhymes *ending in Nasals*. Nasals are always voiced, so they are noticeable. Also, they can be held. (That's what you do when you hum.)

stu*n*	ca*me*	so*ng*
ra*n*	scea*m*	ri*ng*

5. *Masculine* Consonance rhymes ending in *Voiced Fricatives*. Again, these are voiced and can be held.

gra*v*e	ra*ge*	cau*se*
reprie*v*e	ba*dge*	whi*z*

Consonance Rhyme *never* works like Perfect Rhyme. Yet, when it is strong enough, it can work for you. You might use it in a case where you have already committed to a rhyme scheme in an earlier verse, and want to keep it, yet relax the motion in a later verse. In verse two of Paul Simon's "50 Ways to Leave Your Lover" the phrase-end rhymes are

pai*n*
agai*n*
explai*n*

His use of the Consonance rhyme is pretty. The verses are relaxed, both in attitude and structure. The Consonance rhyme in second position dampens the pushing effect of the consecutive rhymes. Try replacing "again" with a Perfect rhyme and see what happens!

Consonance Rhymes are easy to find in the rhyming dictionary. Each vowel sound lists its consonant endings alphabetically. To find a Consonance rhyme for "love," look in each vowel section under "v":

<u>lo*v*e</u>
grave
have
leave
thrive
forgive
rove
groove

EXERCISE 23: FIND SIX RELATED CONSONANCE RHYMES FOR EACH OF THE FOLLOWING WORDS.

1. refusal   _____   _____   _____

   _____   _____   _____

2. forgiven   _____   _____   _____

   _____   _____   _____

3. torch   _____   _____   _____

   _____   _____   _____

4. trail   _____   _____   _____

   _____   _____   _____

5. trance   _____   _____   _____

   _____   _____   _____

6. grasp   _____   _____   _____

   _____   _____   _____

7. tomb   _____   _____   _____

   _____   _____   _____

8. crowned   _____   _____   _____

   _____   _____   _____

9. grove   _____   _____   _____

   _____   _____   _____

10. phrase   _____   _____   _____

   _____   _____   _____

PARTIAL RHYME
From Cradle to Grave

This one is really fun. It rhymes a *masculine syllable* with the *accented syllable of a feminine figure,* leaving the unaccented syllable unrhymed.

Partial Rhyme is the first rhyme type you have seen that is used ONLY for its special effects on structure. Use it to prevent closure in otherwise closed structures. To find it, start with a Feminine figure, then look in the Masculine section to rhyme the stressed syllable. Forget about the unstressed match!

The Feminine figure usually appears first.

In "Why Can't I Have You," Ric Ocasek gets good results using Partial Rhyme to move a verse into a Transitional Bridge:

mo ving

you

He uses the same technique at the end of verse 2:

strik ing

night

Michael Jackson gets the same result in "Billie Jean" with the Partial Assonance rhyme

lov er

one

The Partial Rhyme makes the sound connection, but leaves the structure free to move forward to the final crucial line.

Here are a few more. These are stronger because they use Perfect Rhyme between the stress syllables:

closing	like	steamer
rose	hiking	cream

Look at a word from the earlier section on Family Rhyme. Remember this rhyme search?

travel
bashful
dazzle
wrathful
glass full
satchel
fragile

Add Partial Rhyme:

jazz
laugh
path
Khyber Pass
dash
crash . . . etc.

This really extends your ability to use Feminine words, yet make strong connections between ideas.

EXERCISE 24: FIND THREE RELATED PARTIAL RHYMES FOR EACH OF THE FOLLOWING WORDS. USE ANY RHYME TYPE.

1. love _____ _____ _____

2. serving _____ _____ _____

3. return _____ _____ _____

4. play _____ _____ _____

5. hinting _____ _____ _____

6. farthing _____ _____ _____

7. fetch   _____   _____   _____

8. pullet   _____   _____   _____

9. ring   _____   _____   _____

10. fortune   _____   _____   _____

These more esoteric rhyme types are useful for two purposes,

1. developing strong content for rhyming positions,
2. modifying structural effects

Assonance Rhyme can substitute for Perfect Rhyme, preserving its effects on structure. With Consonance Rhyme and Partial Rhyme, there is no guesswork involved: they WILL affect structure. Use them wisely and sparingly — and make sure they more than pay their room and board by supplying interesting content.

CHAPTER SEVEN
THE FRUITS OF FRIENDSHIP

Now it's time to go back to WORKSHEETS. This time we will launch a full rhyme search. Our goal is to find better words than we did with Perfect Rhyme.
Look again:

> I'm sick of all this risky business
>
> I want to play it safe

For starters, "business" and "safe" can go on the WORKSHEET. You can find rhymes for them.

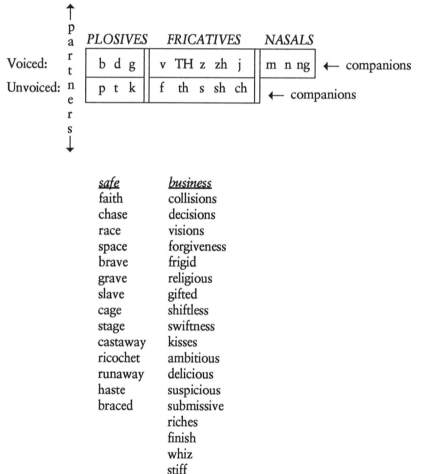

safe	business
faith	collisions
chase	decisions
race	visions
space	forgiveness
brave	frigid
grave	religious
slave	gifted
cage	shiftless
stage	swiftness
castaway	kisses
ricochet	ambitious
runaway	delicious
haste	suspicious
braced	submissive
	riches
	finish
	whiz
	stiff

Better. There are some real possibilities here.

Here is a complete rhyme search for each of the words on the WORKSHEET. Figure out what kind of rhymes they are and how I found them. They are all related to the general idea of "RISKY BUSINESS." The list will have to be trimmed down later.

PERFECT RHYMES	IMPERFECT RHYMES	
1. *scare*	1. *scare*	
affair	compared	
unaware	ensnared	
care	repaired	
dare	snared	
despair	unprepared	
fair	scarce	
glare	stairs	
prayer	airs	
	unfair	
2. *afraid*	2. *afraid*	
charade	bait	wait
fade	date	vague
grade	fate	break
masquerade	gate	awake
parade	hate	earthquake
promenade	late	heartache
	suffocate	rattlesnake
3. *flirt*	3. *flirt*	
alert	absurd	stir
dessert	humming-bird	thirst
dirt	word	burst
hurt	handiwork	worst
inert	jerk	voyeur
introvert	smirk	church
shirt	work	urge
skirt	curb	verge
unhurt	disturbed	preserved
	superb	nerve
	iceberg	reserved
	blur	swerve
	purr	amours
		slurs
4. *attention*	4. *attention*	
apprehension	exemption	complexion
convention	redemption	connection
detention	aggression	direction
intention	confession	infection
invention	discretion	objection
misapprehension	impression	weapon
pretention	obsession	perception
suspension	oppression	clandestine
tension	possession	beckon
	procession	protection
	resurrection	affection
	mend one *etc.*	
	stretchin' *etc.*	

PERFECT RHYMES	IMPERFECT RHYMES	
5. left _out_	5. _out_	
doubt	aloud	renowned
gadabout	cloud	bound
knockout (Id.)	crowd	found
look-out (Id.)	proud	count
scout	allowed	announced
	plowed	denounced
	vowed	trounced
	wowed	aroused
	couch	blouse
	grouch	soused
	drowned	crowned
6. _risk_	6. _risk_	
disc	fist	cliff
(oops!)	kissed	stiff
	mist	tiff
	resist	quick
	tryst	kicks
	wisp	lick(s)
	abyss	sick
	avarice	trick
	bliss	transfixed
	dismissed	ditch
	wished	itch
	dish	pitch
	drift	switch
	gift	bridge
	hints	crypt
	shift	chips
	swift	Apocalypse
7. _chance._	7. _chance_	
advance	avalanche	scram
circumstance	pants	tramp
dance (cliché?)	slants	class
lance	ban(s)	pass
petulance	fans	brash
radiance	plans	flash
	tan	splash
	band	trash
	command(s)	mask
	hand(s)	fast
	jam	last
8. _dull_	8. _dull_	
lull	annulled	diabolical
miracle	gulf	natural
numskull	bulge	physical
spectacle	sulk	ritual
	convulsed	braille
	cult	fail
	insult	stale
	occult	pale
	result	drill
	chemical	brawl
	logical	small

PERFECT RHYMES	IMPERFECT RHYMES	
	(*dull* cont'd)	
	casual	stall
	conjugal	fool
		school

	PERFECT RHYMES		IMPERFECT RHYMES	
9.	*leave*	9.	*leave*	
	believe		breathe	peace
	deceive		seethe	police (Id.)
	grieve		appeased	beach
	ho-heave		please	C.O.D.
			diseased	debris
			freeze	guarantee(s)
			squeeze(d)	knees
			tease(d)	degrees
			prestige	refugee(s)
			relief	amenities
			grief	apologies
			thief	dignity
			teeth	fantasies
			caprice	hostilities
10.	*ignored*	10.	*ignored*	
	adored		court	encore
	bored		support	sore
	deplored		resort	score
	explored		short	roar
	floored		born	troubadour
	gored		torn	porch
	restored		warned	morgue
	scored		forlorn	chord
	outscored		scorned	torch
	sword		deformed	divorce
			storm	poor
			warm(ed)	cured
			reward	endure
			corps	self-assured
11.	*gone*	11.	*gone*	
	chiffon		dawn	
	con		drawn	
	ex-con		beyond	
	echelon		blonde	
	hangers-on		song	
	paragon		wrong	
	put upon		response	
	dying swan			

Rhymes are suggestive. As you look through them, they create associations that can lead you in directions you might not have seen otherwise. A good reason to use WORKSHEETS.

EXERCISE 25: FROM THE COLUMNS OF PERFECT AND IMPERFECT RHYMES ABOVE, CHOOSE YOUR TEN FAVORITE RHYMES FOR EACH OF THE KEYWORDS AND WRITE THEM DOWN BELOW.

1. *scare*

6. *risk*

9. *leave*

2. *afraid*

10. *ignored*

1.	scared
2.	afraid
3.	flirt
4.	attention
5.	left-out
6.	risk
7.	chance
8.	dull
9.	leave
10.	ignored
11.	gone
12.	safe
13.	business

3. *flirt*

11. *gone*

4. *attention*

7. *chance*

12. *safe*

5. *left-out*

8. *dull*

13. *business*

EXERCISE 26: REWRITE YOUR LYRIC "RISKY BUSINESS" USING SOME OF YOUR NEW IDEAS AND RHYME WORDS.

CHAPTER EIGHT
SONIC BONDING

INTERNAL RHYMES

Internal Rhyme is rhyme that happens *inside* of phrases rather than at the ends of phrases. You can use Internal Rhyme to connect ideas, to create acceleration, or, like summer heat lightning, just to create activity. Internal rhymes call attention to themselves, creating "mini" HOT SPOTS.

> Turpen*tine* and dande*lion wine*

> It's *easy* to *please me*

> Got a *fire* in my belly
> Got a *fire* in my head
> Going *higher* and *higher* till I'm dead

Internal rhyme usually has only *local* effects. It does not affect phrase structure and, unlike end rhymes, does not need to be matched in parallel sections. Just put it in your section, let it do its work, then forget about it.

Look at this piece of sonic cotton candy:

> Dance with me my Daisy
>
> Easy lazy days
>
> Wintertime will soon be ending
>
> Hillsides rolling green and plenty
>
> Summertime has come and gone
>
> But she won't stay away
>
> Slip in softly
>
> Catch me napping
>
> Spin your magic, let it happen
>
> Open up and make me smile
>
> these lazy days away

There is so much sound connection in this example that it is hard to know where to stop calling things rhymes. There are a few clear internal rhymes:

> Daisy
> lazy
>
> ha*ppen*
> *Open* } (Feminine Consonance)
> *up an'*

But what about these?

> Ea*sy* la*zy*
> Slip in
> stay away
> lazy days away

You could call them rhymes, but they do not seem to have a rhyming *purpose*. Instead, they seem to be there to make the phrases flow smoothly. Call it Voice Leading.

VOICE LEADING

"Voice Leading" is a musical term. To say a series of chords is "voice led" means that successive chords have one or more notes in common. It makes the chords flow smoothly one to another and sound like they belong together.

In lyrics, VOICE LEADING is called Assonance (having the same vowel sounds) and Alliteration (having the same consonant sounds). They have the same effects as VOICE LEADING in music:

1. They link words together.
2. They make phrases flow more smoothly.

ASSONANCE is a vowel link between syllables. Its purpose is to blend words together — to create smoothness, as in

> lazy days away

> free and easy

The vowel sounds work as guides to slip you from one word into the next. You glide forward to the next position.

Two comments:

1. The line between Voice Leading and Internal Rhyme can be hazy, but one important difference between them is in how they are used. Internal Rhyme is an activator. Assonance Voice Leading is a smoother.

2. Do not mistake Assonance Voice Leading with Assonance Rhyme. When Assonance is used to connect the *ends of phrases,* it has an effect on the lyric structure. Then it is Assonance Rhyme. When it is used as a simple vowel connection INSIDE a phrase — a connection between words rather than phrases, then it is not a rhyme. It is a Voice Leading technique. The effect in

> these l*a*zy d*a*ys aw*ay*

is more a case of Voice Leading than rhyme. Its purpose is to lead you through the words smoothly. It does not create new structures. Nor does it create acceleration.

ALLITERATION means that the words have consonant sounds in common. Sometimes beginning consonants,

> Slip in softly

> Dance with me my Daisy

Sometimes consonants sitting inside words:

> make me smile

> Summertime has come

Be careful of heavy-handed "lap of luxury" Alliteration. It gets old (and distracting) fast. Internal Alliteration is always most effective.

> Hillsides rolling green and plenty

It is hard to escape the feeling that this stuff happens by accident, or by instinct. In fact, it often does. There comes a point where analysis takes more energy than it deserves.

Just as a composer can choose a series of chords because they sound good together (without stopping to ask why), a lyricist can grab a phrase because it sounds "right" or "sings well." It gets silly to point out that "can grab" is Assonance.

A composer can choose to Voice Lead. And so can you. That is another way to use your WORK SHEET. Remember that your WORK SHEET is based on vowel connections. You may find places for many of its words on the insides of your phrases. You only use a small percentage of your WORK SHEET words as end-line rhymes. Put others to work in other places.

Sometimes you can even make Voice Leading help your ideas to work better. Look at this.

> Listen! You hear the grating roar
>
> Of pebbles which the waves draw back, and fling
>
> At their return, up the high strand
>
> *Begin, and end, and then again begin . . .*
>
> — Matthew Arnold, from "Dover Beach"

See how intricately the sounds in the last line are linked to each other. The nasals continue throughout the line. They have a linking effect like a bagpipe drone sound. They glue all the other sounds to a central texture and tone.

All the stressed syllables end in the nasal sound:

> begin, and end, and then again begin

It gives you a feeling of continuous forward motion. The plosives make a more subtle link:

> Begin and end, and then again begin $\rightarrow$

They suggest a cycle.

The three middle vowels also suggest continuous motion. They make you want to start over again too.

> gin *end then gain* gin $\rightarrow$

It works with its meaning at least one way: like waves, it makes you want to keep starting over after you finish.

> Begin and end, and then again begin and end, and
>
> then again begin and end, and then again begin and
>
> end, and then again begin . . .

But the *continuous motion* of the sound (especially the nasals) works directly *against* what it is trying to say. Look again:

> Listen! You hear the grating roar
>
> Of pebbles which the waves draw back, and fling
>
> At their return, up the high strand
>
> Begin, *and end,* and then again begin

The *meaning* of the last line is that the waves' motion comes to a stop — a pause — before continuing on. But the sound does just the opposite! It keeps going without any pause at all!

If you know the poem, you already know that I have mis-quoted it. Here is the real thing:

> Listen! You hear the grating roar
>
> Of pebbles which the waves draw back, and fling
>
> At their return, up the high strand
>
> Begin, and *cease,* and then again begin . . .

What a difference! It is the *break* in the Voice Leading that is expressive.

This example should give you insight into the process of selecting your effects. "End" and "cease" both mean about the same thing. Given these two ways to say the same thing, which word works better? Why?

> Begin, and *end,* and then again begin
>
> Begin, and *cease,* and then again begin

Another question. "Cease" and "stop" both mean about the same thing. Given these two ways to say the same thing, which word works better? Why?

> Begin, and *cease,* and then again begin
>
> Begin, and *stop,* and then again begin

One more. "Cease" and "pause" both mean about the same thing in this context. Given these two ways to say the same thing, which word works better? Why?

> Begin, and *cease,* and then again begin
>
> Begin, and *pause,* and then again begin

Right. "Cease" sounds like ocean waves against the beach!

Matthew Arnold probably did NOT start by saying "I want a word that sounds like the ocean and breaks my Voice Leading expressively." But the selection process led him there.

Moral: put yourself in situations where you have several alternatives, and, provided that you understand how and why to pick, your writing will get better.

EXERCISE 27: USING THE WORKSHEET, WRITE THREE SECTIONS, EACH FOUR PHRASES LONG. IN THE FIRST ONE WORK WITH INTERNAL RHYME TO CREATE ACTIVITY. USE IDEAS APPROPRIATE TO THE ACTIVITY. IN THE SECOND WORK WITH ASSONANCE, AND IN THE THIRD, ALLITERATION (ESPECIALLY INTERNAL ALLITERATION). IN EACH SECTION, RHYME THE PHRASE-ENDS "X A X A."

1.   X a x a rhyme scheme, using internal rhymes within the section:

2.   X a x a rhyme scheme, using Assonance within the section.

3.   X a x a rhyme scheme, using Alliteration within the section:

JUNCTURE

"Juncture" is a term used to describe the way words flow into one another. More precisely, the way the *end* of one word flows into (or fails to flow into) the *beginning* of the word that follows it.

Which article ("a" or "an") do you use with "apple?"

> an apple

Which do you use with "pickle?"

> a pickle

The reason for the difference is to make it easy for you to slide from the article into the noun. You use "an" before a word that starts with a vowel because it gives you a "smooth JUNCTURE." The same for using "a" before a word that starts with a consonant. The rule about English articles is there to make talking easier.

But English doesn't guarantee smooth JUNCTURES. And sometimes they can get you into trouble. Say this aloud:

> She can't take your rent.

Say it to someone who can't see it. Notice the puzzled expression. There are two JUNCTURE problems:

> can't → take
>
> your → rent

The JUNCTURES are "rough" or "staccato." If you try to move through the phrase smoothly, it will sound like

> She can take your ent.

The first part comes out the opposite of what it means. The second part turns into nonsense. To make the meaning clear, you have to pause.

> She can't (pause) take your (pause) rent.

Remember those eyeless ears? Since they are not able to see the words, they can misunderstand. Even if the singer has impeccable diction, he or she will probably spend so much energy just getting the words clear that emotional nuances will be gone.

You must be careful that the phrases you write are singable. One of the main things to watch is JUNCTURE.

When you begin a word with the same sound that *ended* the word before it, you create a staccato JUNCTURE.

> ol*d d*og

One of two things has to happen:

> 1. ol' dog
> 2. old (pause) dog

Either the words sound like an informal "dialect," or the JUNCTURE forces you to pause to make the words clear.

"Old hound" bypasses the problem.

The problem is the same anytime you use the same sound at the end and beginning of consecutive words:

> sa*ve v*ictory
>
> stu*n n*one
>
> fre*e e*ther

The first one will be misunderstood as "say victory." The second will not be understood at all. The third might have a chance, but I doubt it.

You get staccato JUNCTURES even with *sounds of the same family*. Look at these Plosives:

> The ol*d d*og *b*arke*d b*elligerently

Say it a few times. It forces you to pause between words.

Staccato Juncture sometimes (though not often) can be a good thing for a special effect:

> Slicker than a desperado
>
> He moves in smooth and split*s s*taccato

But in general, keep your phrases smooth and singable. The singers of your songs will appreciate it.

THE VOWEL TRIANGLE: BEAUTY AND THE BEAST

It is important for a lyricist to understand vowels and vowel relationships for at least three reasons:

1. To give vocalists comfortable sounds when they approach the upper or lower limits of their ranges.
2. To select vowel sounds that will help vocalists express the emotions of the lyric more effectively.
3. To create more singable lines.

Vowel relationships are illustrated by the "Vowel Triangle":

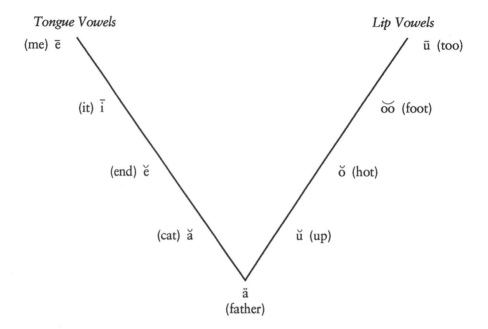

The Vowel Triangle lists vowel sounds according to the way they are formed by the mouth. At the point is "a" (as in "father"), the most open sound. Say "Ahh."

From the point of the triangle, LIP VOWELS move outward along the right leg of the triangle. You form each one in turn by rounding and closing your lips a little more. Your tongue stays out of the way.

TONGUE VOWELS move outward along the left leg of the triangle. You form each one in turn by raising your tongue a little higher toward the roof of your mouth. Your lips stay out of the way, but widen as your tongue gets higher. Try it.

Say "Yeow!" It covers all the vowel positions, from extreme LIP VOWELS to extreme TONGUE VOWELS.

The Vowel Triangle contains *pure* vowel sounds. (A little like Primary Colors.) Now look at the vowels that are not on the Vowel Triangle. They are "dipthongs" ("di" means "two") — combinations of two or more sounds from the Triangle.

a (as in "play")	=	ĕ (as in "end") + ē (as in "me")
i (as in "cry")	=	ə (as in "papa") + ē (as in "me")
o (as in "grow")	=	ŏ (as in "hot") + u (as in "too")
oi (as in "boy")	=	ŏ (as in "hot") + ē (as in "me")
ou (as in couch)	=	a (as in "papa") + u (as in "too")

The nearer to the point of the triangle you are, the easier the vowel is to sing, especially when the notes are at the extreme low or high notes of your range (or, over your "break.") Your throat is more relaxed for these vowels.

Try to use the more relaxed vowels in difficult melodic places, especially when you are writing a lyric to a melody and already know where the difficult melodic spots are. Just another way to use your WORK SHEET.

The long ī is especially interesting as a dipthong. When you sing a dipthong, you hold its FIRST SOUND. Since long ī contains the MOST RELAXED of all English sounds (ä in "father") as its first sound, *it is one of the BEST vowels to sing at across your break, or at either the upper or lower limits of your range.*

Remember this information (or where to find it) when you write lyrics to melodies. It is also helpful when you are setting a lyric, and have to write for an especially low or high note.

Why did I call this section "Beauty and the Beast"? Look at the vowel sounds in the words:

Beauty Beast

They are on extreme opposite ends of the Vowel Triangle:

Tongue Vowels
(me) ē

(it) ī

Lip Vowels
ū (too)

o͝o (foot)

"Beau" is the extreme lip vowel. "Beast" is the extreme tongue vowel.

Here I will risk a generalization and a value judgement. *Lip Vowels are, on the whole, warmer and prettier than Tongue Vowels. Lip vowels are beautiful. Tongue Vowels are beastly.*

Consider a clear (but silly) situation: you are writing and you must choose between

> Hold me tight
>
> Hold me close

Assume that everything else, including rhyme, works out no matter what you choose.

If you are writing a "lust" song, a nasty "I'm–on–the–road–baby–an'–you–ain't–got–nothing–I–want–anytime–but–tonight" song, you would get more emotion out of the Tongue Vowel.

> Hold me tight

If you are writing a romantic song, a warm "I–feel–like–a– newborn–babe–cradled" song, you would get more emotion out of the Lip Vowel.

> Hold me close

Notice also that "hold me close" connects the lovers with the warm bond of long ō Assonance. It is Voice Led.

"Hold me tight" has no such connection. It can move on in the morning with no regrets. No guilty conscience.

Reasons for choosing. Choosing for reasons.

That is the why it pays to study and learn.

AFTERWORD

If you have worked through this book carefully, you are in control of the sounds of your lyric. Your lyrics are better than they were before you started.

Do not be afraid of WORK SHEETS. They take time. But each time they take less time. Each time you do one, the more the process gets inside you. Do them for a while, and you will reach a place where you do most of the work in your head.

Keep using your head. Writing well is never easy. You never have to worry about being able to write as well as someone else. The hardest thing you will EVER do is write as well as YOU can.

Score Compose Arrange

with Berklee Press

berklee press

AS SERIOUS ABOUT MUSIC AS YOU ARE

Songwriting: Essential Guide to Lyric Form and Structure
Tools and Techniques for Writing Better Lyrics

| ISBN: 0-7935-1180-1 | HL: 50481582 | BOOK | $14.95 |

By Pat Pattison

Melody in Songwriting
Tools and Techniques for Writing Hit Songs

| ISBN: 0-634-00638-X | HL: 50449419 | BOOK | $19.95 |

By Jack Perricone

The Songwriter's Workshop: Melody

| ISBN: 0-634-02659-3 | HL: 50449518 | BOOK/CD | $24.95 |

By Jimmy Kachulis

Reharmonization Techniques

| ISBN: 0-634-01585-0 | HL: 50449496 | BOOK | $29.95 |

By Randy Felts

The Songwriter's Workshop: Harmony

| ISBN: 0-634-02661-5 | HL: 50449519 | BOOK/CD | $29.95 |

By Jimmy Kachulis

Music Notation
Theory and Technique for Music Notation

| ISBN: 0-7935-0847-9 | HL: 50449399 | BOOK | $19.95 |

By Mark McGrain

Songwriting: Essential Guide to Rhyming
A Step-by-Step Guide to Better Rhyming and Lyrics

| ISBN: 0-7935-1181-X | HL: 50481583 | BOOK | $14.95 |

By Pat Pattison

Modern Jazz Voicings
Arranging for Small and Medium Ensembles

| ISBN: 0-634-01443-9 | HL: 50449485 | BOOK/CD | $24.95 |

By Ted Pease and Ken Pullig

Essential Songwriter
Berklee In the Pocket Series

| ISBN: 0-87639-054-8 | HL: 50448051 | BOOK | $9.95 |

By Jimmy Kachulis and Jonathan Feist

Arranging for Large Jazz Ensemble

| ISBN: 0-634-03656-4 | HL: 50449528 | BOOK/CD | $39.95 |

By Dick Lowell and Ken Pullig

Jazz Composition: Theory and Practice

| ISBN: 0-87639-001-7 | HL: 50448000 | BOOK/CD | $39.95 |

By Ted Pease

Finale®: An Easy Guide to Music Notation

| ISBN: 0-634-01666-0 | HL: 50449501 | BOOK/CD-ROM | $59.95 |

By Thomas Rudolph and Vincent Leonard, Jr.

The Songs of John Lennon: The Beatles Years

| ISBN: 0-634-01795-0 | HL: 50449504 | BOOK | $24.95 |

By John Stevens

Music Theory

| ISBN: 0-87639-046-7 | HL: 50448043 | BOOK | $24.95 |

By Paul Schmeling

berklee press

Berklee Press books and DVDs are available wherever music books are sold.
Go to www.berkleepress.com or call 866-BERKLEE (237-5533) for a complete catalog of
Berklee Press products.

DISTRIBUTED BY

HAL•LEONARD®

Berklee Press DVDs:
Just Press PLAY

AS SERIOUS ABOUT MUSIC AS YOU ARE

Kenwood Dennard: The Studio/ Touring Drummer
| ISBN: 0-87639-022-X | HL: 50448034 | DVD $19.95 |

The Ultimate Practice Guide for Vocalists
| ISBN: 0-87639-035-1 | HL: 50448017 | DVD $19.95 |

Featuring Donna McElroy

Real-Life Career Guide for the Professional Musician
| ISBN: 0-87639-031-9 | HL: 50448013 | DVD $19.95 |

Featuring David Rosenthal

Essential Rock Grooves for Bass
| ISBN: 0-87639-037-8 | HL: 50448019 | DVD $19.95 |

Featuring Danny Morris

Jazz Guitar Techniques: Modal Voicings
| ISBN: 0-87639-034-3 | HL: 50448016 | DVD $19.95 |

Featuring Rick Peckham

Jim Kelly's Guitar Workshop
| ISBN: 0-634-00865-X | HL: 00320168 | DVD $19.95 |

Latin Jazz Grooves Featuring Victor Mendoza
| ISBN: 0-87639-002-5 | HL: 50448003 | DVD $19.95 |

Basic Afro-Cuban Rhythms for Drum Set and Hand Percussion
| ISBN: 0-87639-030-0 | HL: 50448012 | DVD $19.95 |

Featuring Ricardo Monzón

Vocal Technique: Developing Your Voice for Performance
| ISBN: 0-87639-026-2 | HL: 50448038 | DVD $19.95 |

Featuring Anne Peckham

Preparing for Your Concert
| ISBN: 0-87639-036-X | HL: 50448018 | DVD $19.95 |

Featuring JoAnne Brackeen

Jazz Improvisation: Starting Out with Motivic Development
| ISBN: 0-87639-032-7 | HL: 50448014 | DVD $19.95 |

Featuring Ed Tomassi

Chop Builder for Rock Guitar
| ISBN: 0-87639-033-5 | HL: 50448015 | DVD $19.95 |

Featuring "Shred Lord" Joe Stump

Turntable Technique: The Art of the DJ
| ISBN: 0-87639-038-6 | HL: 50448025 | DVD $24.95 |

Featuring Stephen Webber

Jazz Improvisation: A Personal Approach with Joe Lovano
| ISBN: 0-87639-021-1 | HL: 50448033 | DVD $19.95 |

Harmonic Ear Training
| ISBN: 0-87639-027-0 | HL: 50448039 | DVD $19.95 |

Featuring Roberta Radley

College Credit Online Certificate
Programs And Courses Now Available From
Berklee | music.com™
extension school
Areas of Study Include:
⊙ Production
⊙ Theory, Harmony, & Ear Training
⊙ Songwriting
⊙ Arranging
⊙ Music Business
CALL
1.866.BERKLEE
(237.5533)
to speak with our admissions advisor!
www.berkleemusic.com
Financial Aid Available ⊙ Flexible Schedules ⊙ Study with Berklee Faculty